THE WELSH COB

THE
WELSH COB

WYNNE DAVIES

J. A. ALLEN

British Library cataloguing in publication data
A catalogue record for this book is available from the British Library
ISBN 0 85131 721 9

Published in Great Britain in 1998 by
J. A. Allen & Company Limited
an imprint of Robert Hale Ltd. Clerkenwell House,
45-47 Clerkenwell Green, London, EC1R 0HT.
Reprinted 2000

Edited by Susan Beer
Designed by Paul Saunders
Typeset by Textype Typesetters, Cambridge
Colour separation by Tenon & Polert Colour Scanning (HK) Ltd
Printed in Hong Kong by Dah Hua Printing Press Co. Ltd

Contents

Rhagair

O'R DIWEDD mae croniclwr hanes ein bridiau Cymreig wedi troi ei sylw at Adran D ac mae ei brofiad ar hyd ei oes a chysylltiadau ei deulu a Merlod a Chobiau Cymreig yn ei wneud yn berson delfrydol i'r orchwyl. Yn ystod fy oes i mae'r adran yma wedi datblygu o fod yn frîd dinôd hyd at ei boblogrwydd presennol. Rhaid i ni yn awr ymdrechu i ddiogelu'r nodweddion a ganiataodd iddynt oroesi yn y gorffennol. 'Rwyf bob amser yn rhyfeddu fod rhywbeth a chymaint o egni, harddwch a dewrder wedi ffynni o amgylchfyd garw a hanes anodd. Ond dyma i chi y Cobyn Cymreig a dyma i chi Gymru hefyd.

Rwy'n gwybod y caiff y selogion o'ch plith a'r newydd-ddyfodiaid i'r brîd bleser a mwynhad mawr o'r llyfr yma.

Mary Edwards, Cascob, Sir Faesyfed
Llywydd, CYMCC 1997 – 1998

Foreword

AT LAST THE chronicler of our Welsh breeds turns his attention to the Welsh Cob and his lifetime's experience and family involvement make him the ideal raconteur.

During my own lifetime this section of the Stud Book has evolved from an obscure and dwindling breed to its present popularity. We must now strive to preserve the qualities that allowed them to survive in the past. It never ceases to amaze me that from a harsh environment and a difficult history has developed something of such power, beauty and courage. But that is the Welsh Cob and that is Wales.

I know all you enthusiasts and those who come new to our breed will equally enjoy this book.

Mary Edwards, Cascob, Radnorshire
WPCS President 1997-1998

CHAPTER ONE

A history of the breed

MANY THEORIES have been propounded as to the exact origin of the earliest British horses but, despite much evidence put forward to support these opinions, it is difficult to reach any definite conclusions. Professor Ridgeway in *The origin and influence of the thoroughbred horse* (1905) quotes Caesar who, when he invaded Britain in 55 BC, found that the Belgic tribes occupying the southern regions of Britain employed not only ridden cavalry like the Gauls, but also horses in harness in war chariots. From the sizes of horseshoes and fragments of harness of Roman times Professor Ridgeway concluded that these were ponies under 12 hands rather than horses and that larger animals only appeared between the time of the departure of the Romans from Britain and the arrival of the Normans, when civilisation was gradually advancing, forage and grazing were improving and there had been considerable travelling of humans and animals between Britain and other European countries.

Hywel Dda (Howell the Good) was ruler of Wales in the tenth century and he drew up a code of Welsh laws which held for six centuries; these laws are now housed at the National Library of Wales at Aberystwyth. Hywel Dda described three types of horses in Wales and quoted their values as well as penalties charged to owners of mares and geldings (but not stallions) for damage to crops by trespassing animals or damage to a borrowed horse (if the skin is broken: eightpence or if the hair on its back is fretted: fourpence). Hywel Dda's laws consisted of 120 prelates and 836 deputies from the Commots which were subsequently approved by the Pope.

Prince Hywel, as he was known, was ruler of Deheubarth at the same time as Prince of Gwynedd, Morgannwg and Gwent. In his laws, he wrote of 'three estates of the realm Equine' (in other words, three types of horse):

1. The palfrey, an animal reserved for the delectation of patrician patrons, their pastimes and their pageants, for knights in tournaments, or as ambling hacks dedicated to the use of lords and ladies. Blundeville (a sixteenth-century chronicler) wrote: 'Some have a breed of ambling horses to journey and travel by the way. Some perhaps againe a race of swift runners to runne for wagers, or to gallop the bucke and such exercises of pleasure. But the plaine countryman would perchance have a breed only for draught and burden.'

2. After the ambling horse comes the 'rowncy' or 'sumpter'. *Equus elitellarius* (the animal that carried the pack saddle) was his definition in the days of Giraldus Cambrensis. To the pack horse of the nineteenth century was assigned in fiction the responsibility of bearing illegal burdens in the shape of smugglers' casks and other contraband goods.

3. The *Equus operarius*, the animal who pulled the 'car llysg' or 'gambo', an animal heavier than the present-day Welsh Cob, though not as heavy as the English Shire; horses which in the immediate post-second war Horse Shows in Wales competed as 'Colliers'. Such an animal around 1800 was Black Jack, bred by Mr Pryse Loveden at Buscot Park in Berkshire and brought to Plas Gogerddan in Cardiganshire, where he sired Old Flyer (a strong black horse, a good trotter but blind) who, in turn in 1836, sired Trotting Comet, one of the famous Welsh Cob tap-root sires.

The knight and his destrier was the basic fighting unit of the medieval army and required a minimum of three other horses to keep them in action day after day. If the knight could afford another one, there would be a second destrier because the Great Horse was only ridden in battle. There would be a palfrey for the knight to ride when not in action and a rowncy or cob for the squire to ride while leading the destrier. The rowncy had to travel at a trot because the war horse which the squire was leading was a natural trotter. The palfrey was a pacer and was supplied from the native breeds which were predominantly non-trotting by nature.

Hywel Dda's classification was applicable to Britain as a whole. In

1171 William Fitzstephen described a horse market in London in his *Descriptio Civitatis Londiniae* where the horses fell into six categories:

1. gradarii or 'pacers', the palfreys or street nags;

2. horses suitable for squires, cobs which trot;

3. good quality youngstock of all kinds;

4. pack-horses;

5. war horses, the destriers, known as the 'horses of the right hand' because when not in action they were led by a mounted squire on the off-side of his cob, while the knight took things easy on his palfrey. All destriers trotted and, because it was inconvenient to lead a trotting horse from a pacing horse, the squires were mounted on trotting cobs.

6. brood and draught mares and foals.

In 1188 the crusades were going very badly and the aged Baldwin, Archbishop of Canterbury, toured Wales recruiting soldiers accompanied by Giraldus Cambrenisis (Gerallt Gymro), Archdeacon of Brecon, who wrote his famous *Itinerary through Wales* as they travelled along. In the central district of Wales called Powys, Gerald found 'most excellent Studs' put apart for breeding and deriving their origin from some fine Spanish horses which Robert de Belesme, Count of Shrewsbury, brought into Britain. These Spanish horses were the ancestors of the famous Andalusian breed, which in turn was the ancestor of the modern Lipizzaner and, by their union with Welsh Mountain pony mares, engendered the Welsh Cob which, under the name 'Powis horse', was to provide so many remounts for English armies from the thirteenth century onwards.

A roll of parchment which has been preserved since 1298 is the requisition list for the Falkirk campaign of Edward I and it details 800 horses with the name of the knight or squire to whom each horse was 'on charge', each with its estimated value. All these horses were also divided into four categories:

1. war horses suitable for knights, destriers;

2. rouncies, hard-trotting cobs;

3. 'equi powis' the Powys horses, none other than Welsh Cobs, a type

not available when Fitzstephen classified them in 1171, also ridden by squires;

4. simply called 'horse' which could be either destrier or cob.

Examples from category 3 included:

(a) Robin Fitzpayne has a black Powys cob with white spots, value £16 13s4d;
(b) Sir R. Fitzpayne has a chestnut Powys cob with white feet and star, value £6 and
(c) Robert du Bois, squire to Sir Henry Cantoke, has a Powys cob value £8.

The only blanket-spotted Appaloosa in the whole list of 800 horses was the Welsh Cob, and a very expensive one, probably on account of its colour. All the horses were overvalued compared with open-market prices of the day because the war had been going on for some time and many had been killed and had to be replaced and the estimated value left 'a comfortable profit margin'. Recorded market prices for good-class palfreys in 1299 were £4 to £6 which was much higher than the prices for rouncies.

Among northern cobs there seems to be a predominance of dappled greys and a fair sprinkling of blacks. One of the Welsh Cobs was white, one had an eel stripe, one was dun with a white star. The colour of six of them was not mentioned, presumably since they were of typical Powys horse colour which was chestnut or golden dun and the remaining fourteen are listed as 'pommele' (dappled).

There are many references to the horses of Wales in medieval literature. For example, in the thirteenth century Book of Taliesin (Canu y Meirch) there are references to the 'grey horse of Cunin', 'black horse of Brwyn Wily Breast', 'roan horse of Ceidaw' and 'Shying Dappled Shoulder, the horse of Llemenig'. Poetry of fifteenth-century Welsh poets such as Guto'r Glyn describes horses in Wales at that period and these descriptions would fit the ideal type of Welsh Cob currently in Wales five hundred years later. Guto'r Glyn also refers to the pedigrees of these stallions tracing them back to the stallions of Arthurian and other romances; Wales is probably the only nation in Europe which can refer to the pedigrees of its horses between 1200 and 1600.

Achau'r Ebol
(Allan o waith Guto'r Glyn)

Mab i'r Du, ymhob erw deg,
O Brydyn, o bai redeg;
Merch ei fam i'r march o Fon
Aeth i ddwyn wyth o ddynion.
Mae wyrion i Ddu'r Moroedd,
Gwn mai un onaddun oedd;
Mae yngo nai Myngwyn Ial
Ym Mhowys, nis rhwym hual;
Mae car i farch Ffwg Warin,
A'i gar a fal gwair a'i fin.
Ucha march ei achau ym Mon,
O baladr Talebolion.

Pedigree of a Welsh Cob
By Guto'r Glyn (c. 1445–75)

He is a son of 'Du o Brydyn'
He would win the race in any fair field;
His mother was daughter to the stallion of
Anglesey which carried eight people,
They are descendants to Du'r Moroedd
And I know that he is one of them.
He is nephew to the Myngwyn Ial.
In Powys no fetter could hold him,
He is of the stock of Ffwg Warin's stallion,
And that stock grinds its fodder small
with its strong jaws.
He is a stallion of the highest pedigree
in Anglesey.
From the line of Talebolion.

At about the same time as Blundeville wrote about the palfrey in England, Tudur Aled, a Welshman of gentle birth (uchelwr), wrote several poems in the Welsh language describing stallions.

Here is part of an English translation from Tudur Aled (fl. 1480–1525)

The stallion

He was a river-leaper,
A roebuck's leap from a snake;
He'd face whatever he wished:
If rafter, try to clear it;
There's no need, to make him leap,
For steel against his belly.
With a keen horseman, no clod,
He would know his intention.
If he's sent over a fence,
He will run, the lord's stallion,
Bold jumper where thorns grow thick,
Full of spikes, in Llaneurgain.
Best ever, when set running,
Fine steed to steal a fair girl.
Here awaits me a maiden,
Fair girl, if I have a horse.
For a hind's form what payment
Betters praise of the slim foal?

This poem ('cywydd') emphasises the capabilities of the Welsh Cob in terms of speed of trotting and galloping, ability to jump rivers and carry heavy weights (in one case having carried eight men on his back!). The Welsh farmer needed a horse that could do the farm work and carry him and his wife to market and to church.

As in other parts of Britain and elsewhere in Europe during the eighteenth century, fast trotters came to be prized and the competitive urge among breeders and stallion owners to own the best and fastest trotters came to have an important formative influence on the evolution of the Welsh Cob. Proud stallion owners would challenge other owners to trotting races held on the main road; preachers often became famous, not for the eloquence of their sermons but for the speed of their mounts; sometimes local lads would borrow the preacher's horse while its owner was busily occupied in his pulpit and hold races against the local horses.

ABOVE *A Welsh Cob held by a young man in a buff costume, painted by Thomas Woodward (1835). Courtesy of Sotheby and Co.*

A riding Welsh Cob, signed C B Spalding who exhibited 1840–1849.

The best English trotters in those days were being bred in East Anglia and Yorkshire and often drovers who would walk Welsh Black cattle to the Eastern counties of England would bring back some promising trotting colts or a few mares. It is these prized trotting stallions that have provided us with the earliest records of Welsh Cob blood-lines, notably the stallions, the aforementioned *Trotting Comet* (foaled in 1840) and his son *Welsh Flyer* (foaled in 1861), *True Briton* (foaled in 1830), *Alonzo the Brave* (foaled in 1866) and *Cymro Llwyd* (foaled around 1850). The first four of these were registered in volume I of the Hackney Stud Book (since there was no Welsh Stud Book until 1902) compiled by Henry F. Euren in 1884. The pedigrees of the first three stallions were supplied to Mr Euren by Dafydd (David) Evans of Llwyncadfor, Cardiganshire.

Dafydd Evans was with Trotting Comet when Comet died on 7 February 1861. It was in 1861 that his son, Welsh Flyer, was born and Dafydd Evans bought Welsh Flyer at public auction at the farm where he was born on the death of his breeder, Mr David Davies, Bryngwyn, Llanilar. Dafydd Evans wrote about the pedigrees of Welsh Flyer and his sire, Trotting Comet, in the *Livestock Journal* of 1902.

. . . Trotting Comet, bred by Mr Poole of Peithyll, was by Flyer by Black Jack by Cauliflower, out of his fast chestnut trotting cob mare Bess, she by a colt belonging to a Mr James, Llwyniorweth-isaf, Aberystwyth, he by a horse bought from England by men known at that time as "Bechgyn Bank," the same men as bought Rainbow and other stallions from Yorkshire and other parts of England to Wales. Flyer was bred at Glanmor, Clarach close to Aberystwyth, from a mare working on the farm by a cart horse of that time called Gomer. Flyer was a strong black horse and a good trotter, though blind. His sire, Black Jack, was a Berkshire carter working at Gogerddan, bred at Buscot Park, where the celebrated Buscot Park thoroughbred was bred, which did so much good in Cardiganshire. The Buscot Park estate in Berkshire belonged at that time to Mr Pryse of Gogerddan, and he was farming at Gogerddan and Buscot Park. Trotting Comet, foaled about 1840, was a brown horse with two white legs behind, nice head and neck, long low back, wide hips, rather flat quarters, good legs. Standing, he was a cart horse about 15 1½ in, but going for a short distance he was a flyer and a wonder.

Table 1.1

WELSH FLYER
Brown stallion, 14 hands 3 in
foaled in 1861
Usually known as 'Old Welsh Flyer'
Breeder: David Davies, Bryngwyn, Llanilar
Then owned by Dafydd Evans, Cefncae, Penuwch, Cardiganshire
Prizewinner, e.g. 1st prize at Cardigan Show in 1868.
A stallion with one eye which had an enormous influence on the Welsh Cob breed.
Registered in the Hackney Stud Book, number 856
Described as 'the best trotter in Wales', he was sold by auction for £300.
His Stud card (for 1882) stated that he 'will challenge any stallion of his age (21 years), weight and size (except his sons) to trot for any sum not less than £100'.

— descended from —

TROTTING COMET
Dark brown, 15 hands 1½ in
Foaled in 1840
Died in 1861
Breeder: Mr Poole, Peithyll, Agent of the Gogerddan estate
Owned by Richard Evans, Cefncae, Penuwch
Registered in the Hackney Stud Book number 834

TROTTING NANCY
A well-known trotting mare owned by the Hon. Capt. Vaughan of Crosswood, Aberystwyth

— descended from —

OLD FLYER
Bred at Glanmor, Clarach, near Aberystwyth
Later owned by Mr Pryse Loveden of Gogerddan
A strong black horse, a good trotter but blind

BESS
Mr Poole's celebrated trotting mare

CYMRO LLWYD
Dun, foaled around 1850
Breeder: Mr Jones, Growen, near Merthyr Tydfil
Owned in 1855 by David Williams, Llwyncolfa, Tregaron (uncle, of Dafydd Evans) and in 1864 by Evan Daniel, Cockshead, Llanio Road, Tregaron. Died in 1880.

Unknown

— descended from —

BLACK JACK
Owned by Mr Pryse Pryse of Gogerddan
A light 'cart-horse' (equus operarius)
Sired by Cauliflower

BLACK BESS
By Gomer (a cart horse)

Colt owned by Mr James, Llwyniorwerth Isaf, Aberystwyth

Welsh pony

Arab imported by Mr Crawshay, Cyfarthfa Castle, Merthyr Tydfil

BROWN
Sired by Old Comet Brown out of a mare called Derby by Curry Comb (Thoroughbred)

Unknown

Unknown

The stud card for Trotting Comet (1853) is reproduced courtesy of Mr J. Jenkins, Tonna, Neath and is older than any stud cards appearing in the publication *Welsh Ponies and Cobs* (J. A. Allen, 1980). Mr David Williams, Llwyncolfa, was Dafydd Evans's uncle. The stud card does not explain why the names of the six gentlemen were included at the bottom;

Trotting Comet stud card 1853.

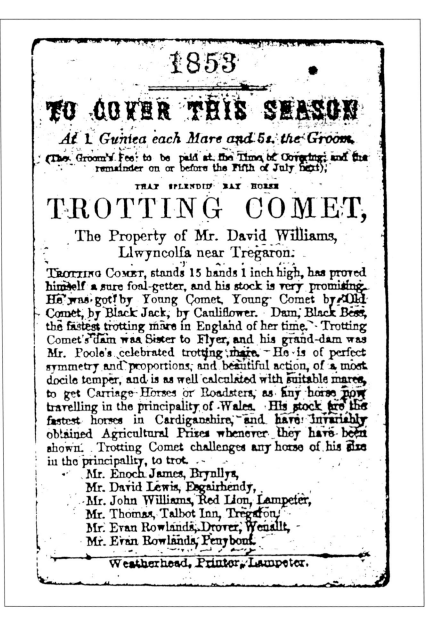

1853

TO COVER THIS SEASON

At 1 Guinea each Mare and 5s. the Groom.

(The Groom's Fee to be paid at the Time of Covering; and the remainder on or before the Fifth of July next);

THAT SPLENDID BAY HORSE

TROTTING COMET,

The Property of Mr. David Williams,
Llwyncolfa near Tregaron:

TROTTING COMET, stands 15 hands 1 inch high, has proved himself a sure foal-getter, and his stock is very promising. He was got by Young Comet, Young Comet by Old Comet, by Black Jack, by Cauliflower. Dam, Black Bess, the fastest trotting mare in England of her time. Trotting Comet's dam was Sister to Flyer, and his grand-dam was Mr. Poole's celebrated trotting mare. He is of perfect symmetry and proportions, and beautiful action, of a most docile temper, and is as well calculated with suitable mares, to get Carriage Horses or Roadsters, as any horse now travelling in the principality of Wales. His stock are the fastest horses in Cardiganshire, and have invariably obtained Agricultural Prizes whenever they have been shown. Trotting Comet challenges any horse of his size in the principality, to trot.

Mr. Enoch James, Brynllys,
Mr. David Lewis, Esgairhendy,
Mr. John Williams, Red Lion, Lampeter,
Mr. Thomas, Talbot Inn, Tregaron,
Mr. Evan Rowlands, Drover, Wenallt,
Mr. Evan Rowlands, Penybont.

Weatherhead, Printer, Lampeter.

possibly they were breeders who had used the services of the stallion and to whom reference could be made, or they were the names and addresses of farmers (some of whom are thirty miles apart) where the stallion would be staying overnight and available for mares to visit the stallion there.

William Hully of Orton owned Comet II, son of Trotting Comet. Comet II trotted a mile in three minutes and he was a very heavy Cob standing 14 hands 3 in. A son of Comet II named Daddy's Lad was so fast that he was bought for Argentina. Mr Charlton's famous Dales stallion Linnel Comet, winner of the championship at the London Pony Show was a son of Daddy's Lad.

One of Welsh Flyer's best sons was Eiddwen Flyer, a 14 hand 2 in chestnut foaled in 1877 and bred by William Jones, Hafodlasuchaf, Llangwyryfon, Cardiganshire. His registration number in the Hackney Stud Book is 2053 (recorded in 1889); his number in the Welsh Stud Book is 421 (recorded in 1911 after he had died in 1902) Eiddwen

Eiddwen Flyer, from the WSB volume I, published after he had died. Photograph courtesy of J Percy Dugdale, Llwyn Stud Farm.

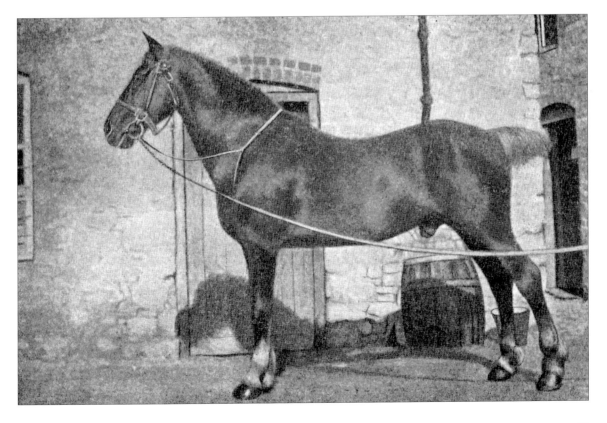

Eiddwen Flyer stud card 1880.

18 80.

TO COVER THIS SEASON,

At One Pound each Mare,

And 2s. 6d. the Groom,

(The Groom's Fee to be paid at the first time of Covering, and the
remainder on or before the 28th of June next,)

THAT SPLENDID CHESTNUT COB,

EIDDWEN FLYER

*The Property of Mr. William Jones, Hafodglas,
Llangwyryfon, Cardiganshire.*

EIDDWEN FLYER is rising 3 years old, stands 14½ hands
high, he was got by Welsh Flyer, which was the fastest
trotter in Cardiganshire; Welsh Flyer by old Comet, old
Comet by Flyer, Flyer out of Brown Bess, Brown Bess by
Black Jack; Welsh Flyer's dam out of Trotting Nancy,
by old Cymro Llwyd. Welsh Flyer won the prize at the
Cardigan Agricultural Show in 1868, and at Llanwrtyd
Entire Horse Show in 1875. EIDDWEN FLYER'S dam was
got by Welsh Jack, the property of Mr. Thomas Daniel,
Caecefnder, Pennant, Cardiganshire, out of Cymro Llwyd,
both of which were excellent trotters. Cymro Llwyd was
the successful Competitor at the Brecon Agricultural Shows
in 1851, 1852, and 1853.

*The Season Money to be paid for any Mare sold
from under this Horse.*

The Groom will specify the time and places of attendance.

PHILIP WILLIAMS, PRINTER, ABERYSTWITH.

Flyer's dam was sired by Welsh Jack, one of the best sons of Cymro
Llwyd, therefore Eiddwen Flyer had two crosses of Cymro Llwyd in his
pedigree.

Roy Charlton in *A Lifetime with Ponies*, writes also of Eiddwen Flyer
and Cymro Llwyd. He starts with Christopher Wilson, the 'founder' of
the Hackney pony breed who lived at Rigmaden Park, Kirkby Lonsdale,
Westmorland. 'Kit' Wilson commenced to make pony history in 1870
when he went right to the top with his Hackneys in a very short time.
By founding the 'Wilson' pony he made himself more famous than any
man who has ever bred ponies in Britain, but he was said to be a strange

Painting of a ridden Welsh Cob (1872), the property of Sir Richard Green Price.

BELOW *A Welsh Cob 'working horse'. Courtesy of Hilltop Studios, Llantrisant.*

13

man with a queer temper. At the height of his glory he decided to sell the lot, could not be persuaded to look at a pony again and devoted his time to trout hatching! The ponies made prices averaging about £1,000, which was an enormous amount for those days. Buyers include Lord Daresbury (then Sir Gilbert Greenall), Sir Humphrey de Trafford and the Marquis of Londonderry. Kit Wilson's groom Bob Moffat went with the best of the ponies to Sir Humphrey de Trafford.

Roy Charlton's father entrusted Roy (when in his early teens) with his cheque book to go to buy any pony which he fancied at the Marquis of Londonderry's Sale on 25 September 1896 and he bought a brood mare for 36 guineas and her colt foal at foot for 12½ guineas. After buying this mare and foal, young Roy Charlton was approached by Bob Moffat who said 'You have made me feel an old fool today. I was sent specially to buy your pony mare for 35 guineas and had to watch a child walk away with the best-bred pony in Britain at just one-tenth of her value. That little mare's dam is Firefly, sired by Cymro Llwyd the "Marshland Shales" of Welsh ponies and cobs and grandsire of the great Eiddwen Flyer.'

The particulars of Cymro Llwyd can be seen in the pedigree of Welsh Flyer, the son of Trotting Comet whose dam, the well-known trotting mare, Trotting Nancy, was sired by Cymro Llwyd (foaled around 1850), who was himself sired by an imported Arab.

Alonzo The Brave was another stallion with which Dafydd Evans had a lasting influence on the Welsh Cob breed, though the stallion had no 'Welsh' blood in his veins. Alonzo was foaled in 1866, bred by Henry Redhead of Leverington in Cambridgeshire. He was a bay horse, standing 15 hands 3 in and of the old Norfolk Trotter blood. Henry Redhead showed the horse at the Royal Show in 1871 and he was bought there by a Mr Powell from Welshpool. In 1874 Alonzo was bought by Dafydd Evans's uncle, Richard Evans, for the enormous sum of £250 and from then until the horse's death at the age of thirty-three, he was travelled through almost every county in Wales. His name appears in the pedigree of 16 of the 70 stallions registered in the first two volumes of the Welsh Stud Book. Tom Jones Evans (Craven Stud), the second of the thirteen children of Dafydd Evans, would relate how he used to drive Alonzo or one of his sons in a light gig around Wales after the covering season to collect the stud fees for all the stallions kept by the family when they later lived at Llwyncadfor. Alonzo The Brave was a typical example of the old Norfolk Cob which resembled the Welsh Cob much more closely in way of trotting than the Arab, Thoroughbred and Yorkshire Coach Horse who, as can be seen here, also had a large contribution into the 'make-up' of the nineteenth-century Welsh Cob.

One of the first of the Norfolk Cobs to be recorded in the Hackney Stud Book was Marshland Shales, a bright chestnut stallion standing 15 hands and foaled in 1802. He was sold in 1807 for 12 guineas to John Chamberlain of Wiggenhall, St Mary Magdalen. George Borrow, who wrote *Wild Wales*, published in 1862, saw Marshland Shales when he was over thirty years old and wrote in his autobiographical novel Lavengro (published in 1851) of how men took off their hats to show respect as Marshland Shales went past.

Marshland Shales (from a painting by E Cooper of Beccles, engraved for the Farmer's Magazine 1823).

Alonzo The Brave, foaled in 1866, was sired by Trotaway (foaled in 1859), whose g-dam Miller's Brown Mare was sired by Black Shales (foaled in 1818) by Marshland Shales (foaled in 1802).

There were a few other Norfolk Cobs which crossed well with Welsh mares at the turn of the century; there were plenty of others, however, whose progeny were disastrous! Examples of the successful ones are:

(1) Trustful, a 15-hand strawberry roan, bred in 1883 by J. Ream of South Brink, Wisbech, Cambridgeshire. Son of the noted D'Oyly's

Black Shales (foaled in 1818),
son of Marshland Shales, bred
by Captain Ogden, Watlington
Hall, King's Lynn. Painting by
William Webb (1780–1846)
formerly in the Ernest Hutton
collection.

BELOW A Norfolk Cob stallion of
the same era as Black Shales.
Painting by Benjamin Herring,
sold at Sotheby and Co on 25th
Feb 1970. This Cob stallion
could represent a Welsh Cob
stallion of the present day but
his contemporary in Wales
(1800–1949) would have had a
docked tail.

Confidence (foaled in 1867), he got his roan colour from his maternal g-sire Great Gun (foaled in 1861). By 1904 Trustful had become the property of the well-known Welsh Cob breeder Mr Tom James, Myrtle Hill, who in 1904 was offering at stud five Hackney stallions, Trustful at 15 hands being the smallest. Trustful appeared at the first Welsh National (now the Royal Welsh) Show on 9 August 1904. He came, was shown, and conquered, and carried away the Welsh Pony and Cob Society medal,

Trustful stud card 1902.

⤙ SEASON 1902 ⤚

Quality, Style, and Actions are the essential points of a good Hackney Horse, and all those qualifications are highly possessed in that magnificent world-renowned

Champion Prize-winning Hackney Stallion

TRUSTFUL

(2741, Vol. VII. H.S.B.)

The Property of Mr. THOMAS JAMES, Myrtle Hill, Llechryd, Cardigan,

(Late of F. W. G. Greswolde Williams, Esq., Strensham Court, Tewkesbury. Bred by J. Ream, Esq., South Brink, Wisbeach, Norfolk.)

Will serve Mares this Season at £3 0s. each Mare ; Tenant Farmers, £2 0s., and 5s. the Groom.

(The Groom's Fee to be paid the first time of serving, and the remainder on or before the 25th of June next, or 5s. extra for collecting.)

Route and places of attendance will be specified by the Groom.

Neither the Groom or the Owner will be responsible for any accident which may occur to mares, but all care shall be taken.

All mares tried and covered by another, sold, exchanged, dead or otherwise disposed of, or not come forward, will be charged full price.

☞ For further particulars apply to the Owner.

M. M. AND W. R. THOMAS, STEAM PRINTERS, CARDIGAN.

despite the fact that there was not a single teaspoon of Welsh blood in his veins.

The roan colour from Trustful survived many generations in Cardiganshire, the black Gerynant Rosina (foaled in 1955) and dam of the famous Synod William, Synod Cerdin, etc. was herself daughter of the roan Dyffryn Rosina (foaled in 1938 and dam of the Royal Welsh champions Lyn Cwmcoed and the roan Lili Cwmcoed), Dyffryn Rosina being a daughter of the roan Myrtle Rosina (foaled in 1925 and champion at the 1938 Royal Welsh Show) whose dam, the roan Myrtle Lady Trustful (foaled in 1902) was sired by Trustful.

(2) Dilham Confidence, a 15-hand brown stallion, foaled in 1886, bred by W. G. Fryer, Browick Hall, Wymondham, Norfolk, was again sired by D'Oyly's Confidence. He was successful in the London Hackney shows and his stock sold well; for example, Dilham Prime Minister sold to the United States for 1,000 guineas. In 1902 Dilham Confidence came to the Llwyncadfor Stud and his stock soon became formidable in the show ring. For example, the top five in the two-year-old class at Knighton Show in 1906 were all sired by him; also some of his sons were kept entire, one of these being Dilham Confidence II (foaled in 1905) and owned by Hugh Hughes, Tymawr, Llanfihangel-y-Creuddyn.

(3) Honesty, foaled in 1877 and bred by J. Grout, Woodbridge, Suffolk. Another of the stallions standing at Llwyncadfor, he sired Woodcock who in turn sired Pride of the Hills, the first recipient of the Prince of Wales Cup in 1908 (chapter 2).

(4) Evolution, a chestnut stallion, foaled in 1886, bred by John Rutter of Cambridge. He became the property of Mr R. T. Hawkins of Builth Wells in 1897, and his influence was more on the Breconshire Cob than on the Cardiganshire Cob. One son, Evolve (foaled in 1898), was g-sire of the 1924 and 1925 Prince of Wales Royal Welsh Cup winner Mathrafal Brenin.

The examples quoted here are just four of about fifteen to twenty 'hackney' stallions who could almost be passed as Welsh Cobs, their progeny being very useful animals, registered in the Welsh Stud Book. There would have been another hundred or more in Wales in the second half of the last century that were useful, inasmuch as their progeny could be sold as smart 'show off' harness horses for the gentry for sufficient

D'Oyly's Confidence, the most influential of the Norfolk-bred Hackneys.

Evolve, foaled in 1898. Grandsire of the 1924 and 1925 Royal Welsh Show Champion Mathrafal Brenin.

money to feed the farmer's family but of no improvement to the Welsh Cob breed. Fortunately there were sufficient diehard breeders in Wales who stuck to the old 'Welsh' type which had been formulated in the first half of the century and before.

The last of the most influential tap-root sires of the early nineteenth century was *True Briton*, foaled in 1830. His sire, Ruler, was a Yorkshire Coach horse and his dam was a Welsh mare, Douse, sired by True Briton Trotter, who himself was sired by Granby, a Thoroughbred registered in the General Stud Book, out of the chestnut trotting mare Flower by Flower of England. Old Douse, dam of Douse, was described by Mr Charles Coltman Rogers as an 'Arab mare bought from the gipsies' but her painting by Sawrey Gilpin RA shows a typical Welsh Cob type and not an 'Arab mare bought from gipsies'! The painting of Old Douse, g-dam of True Briton, painted by Sawrey Gilpin RA (1803) appeared in the book *Two hundred years of British farm livestock* by Stephen J. G. Hall and Juliet Clutton-Brock of the British Museum of Natural History (formerly in the Ernest Hutton collection). Douse and Old Douse are recorded in the Hackney Stud Book as having been bred by John Walters of Llanfair Clydogau, Cardiganshire, who at that time was agent to Lord Carrington's extensive estates in that area. John Walters also bred both True Briton and True Briton Trotter, but True Briton was sold as a three-year old to Thomas Jones, a stonemason on New Court, Lampeter, and True Briton was affectionately known throughout Wales as 'ceffyl du Twm Masiwn' – the black horse of Tom the Mason.

In an attempt to trace the origin of the Welsh Cob, the Hackney, or any similar type, it must be remembered that none of these breeds is, in the true sense of the word, pure. There can be no doubt that the so-called roadsters or Cobs were more or less admixtures of varieties. Already we have met Trotting Comet with his 'cart horse' grandsire Black Jack; Welsh Flyer's grand-sire Cymro Llwyd, who was sired by an imported Arab; the Hackney Alonzo the Brave and True Briton, sired by a Yorkshire Coach horse. Dafydd Evans, writing in the *Livestock Journal* in 1902, writes that he 'has never seen a pure-bred Welsh Cob although I have been judging at different Shows in ten out of the twelve Welsh Counties and have taken first prizes with stallions in ten Welsh Counties'.

There comes a day in the history of all breeds when the blend, after being persevered with, becomes a type to which is given a distinctive title. In this way the Welsh Cob, having been inbred for some generations became known universally as the Welsh Trotting Cob.

With the Welsh Cob breed having become more-or-less stabilised at the end of the nineteenth century along the lines of the animals described in the poetry of Tudur Aled four hundred years previously, crossing typical Cob mares with Hackneys or Shires to produce offspring which fetched greater returns when sold depleted the breed of animals which were already in short supply. Crossing with Hackneys of the sort of Alonzo the Brave did not produce irrevocable damage; the progeny had quality but not constitution and stamina of the old Welsh Cob. The Shire or Collier, however, brought in coarseness, a big head with a roman nose and flopping lower lip and thick bone of poor quality and clumsiness. When the Welsh Pony and Cob Society was started in 1902, the main aim was to encourage the breeding of the 'pure' Welsh Cob. Sections C and D of the first volumes of the Welsh Stud Book were devoted to (C): Welsh Cobs between 13 hands 2 in and 14 hands 2 in and (D) between 14 hands 2 in and 15 hands 2 in. We see from early stud cards that many Welsh Cob stallions of pre-Stud Book times were over 15 hands 2 in – for example, Cardigan Comet III (foaled in 1880) was 15 hands 3 in and Cardigan Comet IV (foaled in 1885) was 16 hands. At the 1905 AGM of the WPCS the question of the upper height limit for section D was discussed and Mr Davies of Caersws stated that the farmers of his area regretted that the upper height limit had ever been instituted; he was supported by three great authorities of the breed, Dafydd Evans of Llwyncadfor, Sir Richard Green Price and Mr Marshall Dugdale of Llanfyllin and the motion was carried to abolish the upper height limit of 15 hands 2 in. In fact in volume I of the Welsh Stud Book there were ten stallions registered in Section C and more (twelve) in Section D; similarly with the females.

In order to encourage the breeding of Cobs without alien blood, the Prince of Wales offered a silver challenge Cup in 1908 to be competed for at the Welsh National Show (now the Royal Welsh Agricultural Society Show) for the 'best Welsh Cob of the Old Welsh Type from four to seven years old'. This competition now engenders the same excitement as is experienced at a rugby international match and is the subject of chapter 2.

Mr Coltman Rogers who had always stressed the importance of keeping to the true Welsh type, must have received great comfort when HRH The Prince of Wales presented his trophy for Cobs 'of the Old Welsh type' in 1908 and further support when the WPCS on 2 February 1912 received a letter from Mr T. H. Elliott, Secretary of the Board of Agriculture and Fisheries, announcing that the Board would offer premiums of £50 each (equivalent to today's £2,000) to Welsh Cob stallions of the 'old Welsh Stamp' who would be required to serve twenty-five mares each.

Most of the discussion at the Annual General Meeting of the WPCS held on 31 August 1913 under the chairmanship of Alderman Charles

Driving Cobs of the gentry at Brynhyfryd, Dolgellau (courtesy of Gwynedd Archives Service).

Coltman Rogers centred around the purity of the Welsh breeds, both pony and Cob. Many members complained that prize money and silver medals donated by the Society were being awarded to pure-bred Hackneys who had been entered in the Welsh Stud Books just so that they could compete at Welsh Shows. The case of the 1913 Knighton Show was quoted where 'Hackneys had it from beginning to end'; in the stallion class the first prize was awarded to Tregaron Horace, one of the most pure Hackneys in existence. The horse placed second had Hackney blood but the third was a 'pure Welsh horse'. One suggestion made was that all entries for the Welsh National Show should be forwarded to the WPCS before the Show date, a small committee would carefully examine the pedigrees of the animals entered and refuse any that were not satisfactory. On a division, this motion was carried. On a cheerful note, the Secretary Mr J. R. Bache reported that 238 more entries had been received for volume 12 of the Welsh Stud Book than in the preceding volume and that the expediency of closing the Stud Book to any but the produce of registered stock might arise.

Mr Coltman Rogers, who was the representative of Wales upon the Board of Agriculture Commission, reported that the Commission was strongly in favour of a monetary scheme to enable Pony Associations to govern the breeding of ponies on Common Lands and that they were 'making great efforts to further the interests of the old Welsh breed of roadsters or cobs. The Board had announced their intention to subsidise none other than the strictly national breed.' No encouragement in the way of premiums was to be given to immigrant Hackneys in Wales or Welsh Cobs in Norfolk.

The board of Agriculture Report (Industry: HB 1912) stated 'In Pembrokeshire and Carmarthenshire, schemes have been set on foot for the revival of the old Welsh Light Cart Horse or Roadster Breed, which, as a distinct breed is rapidly disappearing.' £400 each was allocated to these two County Committees to purchase suitable mares and provision was also made for the acquisition of stallions to mate with such mares.

Without entering upon any vexed question as to what was a Roadster or what is a Cob, it was true that in Pembrokeshire and in parts of Carmarthenshire, possibly as a result of climatic influences or general environment, there was a bigger type of composite bred animal. The three stallions acquired by these two County Committees were Plynlimmon Champion (by Express Comet by Cardigan Comet ex a mare by Eiddwen Flyer), Welshman (previously called Lord Nelson by Briton Flyer ex Lady Elsie of germane Welsh breeding) and Cerdin Briton (by Young Briton out of Cerdin Bess by Caradog out of Bess by Old Comet), all three stallions tracing back to the old Cardigan Trotting Comets and Welsh Flyer.

The Light Horse Breeding Report continues: 'Steps are also being taken to encourage the revival of the breeding of the old strain of Welsh Cob.' In this case no grant had been made for the purchase of mares but a limited number of premiums for Welsh Cob stallions are to be awarded by the Board which will allow of the free service of these Cobs being given to not more than twenty-five mares of the breed. Five Welsh Cob stallions were awarded premiums of £50 each in 1912.

For the first time, in the Welsh Stud Book volume 13 (1914), regulation (g) applied: 'No Pony or Cob eligible for entry in the Hackney Stud Book will be accepted for entry in the Welsh Stud Book unless its sire and dam are entered in a previous volume of the WSB.' There were however, enough pure Hackney stallions and mares already registered to enable 'pure hackneys' to be eligible for registration for a few more generations.

Most of the registrations in volume 13 were entered under regulation (e) which was 'The produce of a Registered sire and from a Registered dam shall be eligible for entry.' There were some animals however, of obvious typical Welsh type, which were allowed into the Stud Book under regulation (f) i.e. other animals which are recommended for entry by Inspection judges; these were mainly the progeny of registered sires out of typically Welsh (though not registered) mares. When the 'foundation stock' scheme was introduced in 1930, unregistered mares had to be registered as FS after inspection. Their male progeny could not be registered but the female progeny could be up-graded i.e. first generation by a registered sire after inspection became FS1, the next generation similarly became FS2 from which both male and female progeny by registered sires automatically went into the 'Stud Book proper'.

The 'foundation stock' scheme had a greater impact on Welsh Cob breeding than on pony breeding. At the end of the second world war there were only about ten Cob stallions and twenty-five Cob mares left in the whole Stud Book whereas there were ten times this number of mountain ponies. When the first premiums were offered (see chapter 3) there were sufficient, if not plentiful, Welsh Cob mares available to take up the offer of free services to premium stallions. The famous equestrian artist Lionel Edwards, who served in the Army Remount Service in the First World War, recalled how he saw hundreds of Welsh Cob mares commandeered into the war effort being unloaded in Salonica never to return. Also during the agricultural depression years of the thirties, many breeders were unable to pay the registration fees and the progeny of these worthy mares then had to start all over again as FS then FS1 and FS2 before being accepted into the Welsh Stud Book after the second war. There was a ready market for harness Cobs, whether registered or unregistered for pulling the milk carts in the big English cities with representatives of such as the United Dairies coming to Cardiganshire to purchase them, dozens at a time.

The Secretary of the WPCS in the lean period (he was also Secretary of the Royal Welsh Agricultural Society) was Captain T. A. Howson and he left no stone unturned in persuading owners to register their animals. An interesting comparison of volume of registrations via the FS scheme of Welsh Cob compared with their pony counterparts is to quote the numbers of Royal Welsh Show champions of these two sections for the years 1947–94 (the FS scheme was discontinued when numbers became viable in 1950; there were no FS breeding mares remaining in 1980 and only thirteen FS1 mares still breeding in 1990).

While only two male and four female section A Royal Welsh champions were progeny of FS2 mares, many of the most famous Royal Welsh Cob champions owe their eligibility to the Foundation Stock pathway: animals such as Brenin Gwalia, Meiarth Welsh Maid, Llwynog-y-Garth, Pentre Eiddwen Comet, Dewi Rosina, Sheila, Teifi Welsh Maid, Llanarth Brummel, Geler Daisy, Derwen Rosina and Llanarth Flying Comet.

The most influential Cob stallion in terms of siring Royal Welsh Show champions during these same years (1947–94) was Mathrafal, foaled in 1936 and sired by Mab-y-Brenin, who was owned by my grandfather. Mathrafal sired four male champions (Llwynog y Garth, Cefn Parc Boy, Pentre Rainbow and Tyngwndwn Cream Boy) and two female champions (Parc Lady and Tyhen Mattie) representing a total of thirteen championships between them. Next influential sires (equal with eleven championships each) are Pentre Eiddwen Comet (with three male champions Tyhen Comet, Nebo Black Magic and Llanarth Flying Comet and one female champion Geler Daisy) and Cahn Dafydd (with one male champion Brenin Dafydd and three female champions Derwen Rosina, Parc Rachel and Cathedine Welsh Maid). The recovery made by the Welsh Cob breed in the last fifty years is indicated by the numbers of registrations in the Welsh Stud Book.

It is seen from table 1.2 on p.26 that the number of Welsh Cob mares which denotes the gene pool available for breeding has increased from eighteen per year in volume 32 to 128 per year in 1965 and 1,157 per year in 1996. The FS avenue, which served a very useful purpose in the forties and fifties to supply the gene pool is no longer necessary and upgrading has worked its way through the system.

In the last thirty years the percentage of Welsh Cobs as compared with total registrations has increased ten-fold, Welsh Mountain pony registrations (section A) during the same period have decreased from 58 per cent. The ten-fold increase in cob gelding registrations is also encouraging, brought about largely by the high prices obtained for reliable performance geldings at the Society Sales and the successes achieved by geldings against all other breeds for riding and driving etc.

Table 1.2 Registrations in the Welsh Stud Book 1939–1996

WSB volume	Welsh Cob stallions	mares	FS mares	geldings	total Cobs	Total of all sections	Welsh Cobs % of total Welsh registrations
32 (ten years 1939–1948)	49	118	57	7	231	978	23
49 (one year 1965)	68	104	24	51	247	6427	3.8
71 (one year 1990)	657	833	6	262	1758	5197	34
77 (one year 1996)	956	1157		627	2740	8377	33

The same growth is reflected in the in-hand Welsh Cob entries at the Royal Welsh Show, total numbers which did not exceed fifty for the years 1904 to 1970 were increasing at the rate of an additional fifty per cent during the eighties to stabilise at around 550 in the late nineties.

year	number of entries
1947	26
1957	29
1967	83
1977	106
1982	211
1987	335
1992	461
1997	536

Numbers in the harness classes have remained virtually constant during the last twenty years. The most dramatic increases have been experienced within the ridden Cob classes with numbers increasing from around ten in one class in 1970 to 154 in three classes in 1997; these high numbers necessitated an increase in the number of classes to six in 1998.

The description of the Welsh Cob found in the poetry of Tudur Aled in the sixteenth century was reiterated by Captain Howson (Secretary of the WPCS from 1928 to 1948) as follows:

> As its very name implies, a Welsh Cob must be a short legged animal of Herculean strength. In build it is distinctly the dual-purpose ride and drive type, combining quality activity, and a spirited yet kindly temperament with a subtle 'personality' entirely its own. It may be anything from something under 14 to something over 15 hands in height and shows much pony character all over, but especially about the head and forehand and in the silky forelock, mane and heel tufts. Viewed from the front, a Cob should display some width of chest and from behind the thighs must be extremely powerful and full – a split-up, stilty cob is an abomination. It must walk quickly and collectedly and its trotting paces must be very forceful, free and fast, with every joint in use. It must get away in front with full play of the shoulders, knees well up, then forelegs straightened out and feet brought lightly to the ground, without the slightest tendency to drop upon the heels. The hocks must be flexed vigorously and the hind legs switched electrically beneath the body in order to support the weight, give proper balance, and provide propulsive power. The action should be straight and true all round, although a few exceptionally fast trotters are inclined to go a trifle wide behind.

and this is altered very little in today's official description:

General character
Strong, hardy and active, with pony character and as much substance as possible.

Colour
Any colour, except piebald and skewbald.

Head
Full of quality and pony character. A coarse head and Roman nose are most objectionable.

Eyes
Bold, prominent and set widely apart.

Ears
Neat and well set.

Neck
Lengthy and well carried. Moderately lean in the case of mares, but inclined to be cresty in the case of mature stallions.

Shoulders
Strong but well laid back.

Forelegs
Set square and not tied in at the elbows. Long, strong forearms. Knees well developed with an abundance of bone below them. Pasterns of proportionate slope and length. Feet well-shaped. Hooves dense. When in the rough, a moderate quantity of silky feather is not objected to but coarse, wiry hair is definitely objected to.

Middlepiece
Back and loins, muscular, strong and well-coupled. Deep through the heart and well-ribbed up.

Hind quarters
Lengthy and strong. Ragged or drooping quarters are objectionable. Tail well-set on.

Hind legs
Second thighs, strong and muscular. Hocks, large, flat and clean, with points prominent, turning neither inwards nor outwards. The hind legs must not be too bent and the hock not set behind a line falling from the point of the quarter to the fetlock joint. Pasterns of proportionate slope and length. Feet well-shaped. Hooves dense.

Action
Free, true and forcible. The knee should be bent and the whole foreleg should be extended straight from the shoulder and as far forward as possible in the trot. Hocks flexed under the body with straight and powerful leverage.

CHAPTER TWO

The George Prince
of Wales Cup

A S ALREADY MENTIONED in chapter 1, many prominent
breeders in Wales at the turn of the century were becoming
alarmed at the increasing influence of Hackney blood on the
Welsh Cob breed. Lord Lucas, in his annual report to the New Forest
Pony and Cattle Society (1908) wrote 'We have so far in the New Forest
been spared the far more dangerous (because more specious and showy)
cross with the Hackney. The Cob in Wales has been practically
obliterated by the introduction of Hackney blood. Its place has been
taken by an ungainly animal which has neither the polish of the Hackney
nor the wiry staying power of the breed which it has superseded. We
cannot afford to graft on to our breed the loaded shoulder or the thick
neck or the congenital softness of this pampered breed.'

Lord Lucas's sentiments turned out to have been too pessimistic and
fortunately there was a gene pool of the old Welsh Trotting Cob still
available in Wales and some of the crosses with the Norfolk Hackneys
(the cobby sort such as D'Oyly's Confidence as distinct from the
Yorkshire higher-stepping lighter-boned variety such as Denmark,
Fireaway and Lord Derby II) produced very commendable animals of
which Wales was justifiably proud.

In order to encourage the breeding of Welsh Cobs of the 'old Welsh
stamp' HRH George, Prince of Wales, in 1908 donated a Silver
Challenge Cup (value 50 guineas, equivalent to about £2,500 today) to
be competed for annually at the Welsh National Show (now the Royal
Welsh Show) for the best Cob of the old Welsh type, between four and
seven years old, not under 14 hands or over 15 hands, bred and owned by
a bone-fide resident within the Principality of Wales or Monmouthshire

and entered in the Welsh Stud Book. The restrictions of age and height were discontinued in about 1925 and the 'residence and breeding in Wales' deleted in 1968.

Competition in the Welsh Cob classes at the Welsh National Show in those days was top-heavy with pure Hackneys; of the nine stallions, five mares and twenty-four youngstock entered in 1905, six of the stallions were pure Hackneys bred by some of the leading breeders of the day: Sir Gilbert Greenall of Walton Hall, Warrington, Sir Frederick Ripley, Hanley Castle, Worcester, A. S. Day of Berkeley Towers, Crewe, A. W. Hickling, Adbolton, Nottingham and others. Similarly, more than half of the mares and youngstock were also pure Hackneys, including some which had won at the London Hackney Shows.

This situation continued in 1906 and 1907, the winners including Viscount Tredegar's Melton Cadet, C. W. Powell's Clara Botherem, C. Lloyd-Edwards's Berkeley George, and A. E. Darby's Lady Abington – all pure Hackneys, despite the judges being the two Welsh Pony and Cob stalwarts Mr W. S. Miller of Forest Lodge, Brecon and Mr J. R. Bache of Knighton.

In 1908 the judge of the Open Welsh Cob classes was the Hackney expert Mr William Foster of Mel Valley and understandably the pure Hackneys swept the board, the stallions Atwick Junior, Mark Well, Kassimede, Clyde Valley Relish (owned by Mr Ernest Hutton of Eye, Suffolk whose paintings are included in this book), Warburton Aneroid, Tissington Goss all exhibited with their Hackney Stud Book registration numbers and the mares Dafydd Evans's famous Hackneys Norton Sceptre and Naughty Naiad and the London Hackney Show champion Merry Polly owned by the Tanrallt Stud, where my sister now lives. These Hackneys had a dual registration in the Welsh Stud Book so that they could compete for WPCS medals, the overall male medal going to Atwick Junior (though the perfect Mountain Pony stallion Greylight was present) and the female medal to Norton Sceptre.

The judge of the George Prince of Wales Cup competition fortunately was not Mr Foster but Sir Richard Green-Price, a great enthusiast of the Old Welsh breed and avid student of their pedigrees. Had the cup been awarded to a pure Hackney bred within the Principality registered in the WSB technically no one could have objected, though it would have been a misconstruction of intent of the donor. As it turned out, the first recipient of the George Prince of Wales cup was the Aberystwyth-owned mare Pride of the Hills (foaled in 1902) who had stood bottom of her class under Mr Foster. This mare could claim her 'Welshness' even if one of her grandsires was a bit of a foreigner, the other was Welsh to the core, so also were both of her grand-dams. Analysis of her pedigree reveals Pride of the Hills to be three-quarters Welsh, one-eighth Hackney and one-eighth Thoroughbred.

Pride of the Hills, foaled in 1902, the first recipient of the George Prince of Wales Cup in 1908, ridden by her owner/breeder, Mr H P Edwards, Lovesgrove, Aberystwyth.

Not only did Woodcock receive fame as the sire of the first recipient of the George Prince of Wales Cup but also as one of the founder sires of Connemara ponies in Ireland. Purchased by the Congested Districts Board of Ireland as a premium stallion for the Galway District, he won first prize at Galway in 1901 and stayed on at Clifden after the CDB gave up responsibility for the stallions in 1903.

Of the sixteen stallions and mares entered for the Prince of Wales Cup competition in 1908, only two could be classified as strictly 'Welsh', that is, at least as far back as the half-Arab Cymro Llwyd (foaled around 1850), the half Yorkshire coach horse, True Briton (foaled in 1830) or the quarter cart horse, Trotting Comet (foaled in 1861). These were the mare, Cwm Eiddwen Rosie, foaled in 1904, owned and bred by Messrs Pugh of Pencwmawr, Llanrhystyd, and sired by Young Messenger (same sire as the noted Klondyke owned by my grandfather's uncle John Thomas of Tre'rddol, who was not quite 14 hands and consequently could not compete) by Eiddwen Flyer II by Eiddwen Flyer. Eiddwen Rosie's dam Cwm Beauty of Eiddwen was also by Eiddwen Flyer and her g-dam was by Welsh Jack. Eiddwen Rosie was reserve to Pride of the Hills and standing third was the other Welshman, the six-year-old stallion High Stepping Gambler II who won the trophy the following year with E.

Table 2.1 PRIDE OF THE HILLS WSB 1411

Owner and breeder Mr H. P. Edwards, Lovesgrove, Aberystwth

- **WOODCOCK WSB 38 foaled 1892**
  - HONESTY HSB 370 (Grout's) foaled 1877
    - HONESTY HSB 369 (Farrer's) foaled 1874
      - CONFIDENCE (D'Oyly's) HSB 158
        - PRICKWILLOW HSB 614
        - LANDLOR
      - Brown mare
        - by ROBIN HOOD by SHALES
    - Brown mare
      - LAMPLIGHTER (TB)
      - Hackney mare
  - BAL II WSB 507
    - CARADOG foaled 1872
      - WELSH JACK Stud card WP&C p. 289
        - CYMRO LLWYD foaled 1830
        - Bay mare by OLD COMET
      - Welsh mare
        - CARDIGAN COMET
        - STAR by OLD BRITON COMET
    - BAL I
      - TROTTING BRITON Stud card WP&C p. 283
        - BRITON COMET by TROTTING COMET
      - STAR

- **BLACK BESS WSB 1315 foaled 1890**
  - WELSH FLYER IV 6613 HSB foaled 1883
    - WELSH FLYER III 4074 HSB foaled 1877
      - WELSH FLYER 856 HSB foaled 1861
        - TROTTING COMET foaled 1840
        - TROTTING NANCY
      - BLAZE
        - OLD CONFIDENCE
        - Welsh mare by GAMBLER
    - POLLY II HSB10420 foaled 1875
      - ALONZO THE BRAVE HSB 22 foaled 1866
        - TROTAWAY 833 HSB
        - Mare by PREMIER
      - POLLY I foaled 1861
        - TROTTING COMET 834 HSB
  - Welsh mare
    - BRITON COMET
      - TROTTING COMET HSB 834 foaled 1836
        - FLYER by BLACK JACK
        - BESS
      - Welsh mare
        - YOUNG COMET
    - Welsh mare
      - --
      - --

Rosie reserve. High Stepping Gambler II was sired by High Stepping Gambler I by Welsh Briton by Old Briton Comet by Old Trotting Comet (foaled in 1840). Gambler's dam was Darby by Caradog by Welsh Jack by Cymro Llwyd (foaled around 1850). In 1908 and 1909 High Stepping Gambler II was still owned by his owners/breeders Messrs Evan and David Davies, Penrhiw, Silian, Lampeter who later sold him to their nephews Harry and David Rees; David Rees's grandson Roderick Rees winning the same trophy in 1993!

Of the remaining thirteen animals competing for the Prince of Wales Cup in 1908, six were half Hackney, half Welsh and seven were pure Hackneys. Of the sixty-eight Welsh ponies and Cobs entered for the 1908 Show, eighteen were described as 'For Sale by Auction' including High Stepping Gambler II.

Woodcock (sire of Pride of the Hills) foaled in 1892, g-g-g-son of Cymro Llwyd (foaled in 1830).

❋ SEASON 1901 ❋

THE COB STALLION,

WOODCOCK,

(Winner of the North Cardiganshire Association Prize, 1897)

The Property of Mr. JOHN JONES, Rhiwlug, Tregroes, Llandyssul,

Will Serve Mares this Season at £2 2s. each Mare, and 5s. the Groom.

*Groom's Fee to be paid at the first time of serving, and the remainder
on or before the 24th June next.*

WOODCOCK is a beautiful brown horse, rising 9 years old, stands 15 hands high, with grand action and of perfect symmetry and proportion, possesses the best legs, and free from hereditary unsoundness. WOODCOCK's sire, Honesty Grouts', No. 370 in H.S.B., is the winner of over 20 First and Second Prizes, including the Royal Agricultural Society of England. He was bred by John Grouts, Esq., of Woodbridge, Suffolk, and sold, when a two-year-old, for 200 guineas. One of his offspring won the Royal Manchester and Liverpool Prize at Wellington, and was sold for £400 for export.

Honesty, 370, is by Honesty (Farrer's), 369, by (D'Oyley's) Confidence, 158, by Prickwillow, 229. His dam, a brown mare, by Lamplighter, by Phosphorus. The dam of Phosphorus was a mare bought of Lord Westmoreland by the Marquis of Hereford. She trotted 17 miles in 55 minutes 53 seconds; and bred two daughters, each of which trotted 14 miles in 48 minutes 3 seconds. (See *Appendix to Volume I. in H.S.B.*)

WOODCOCK's dam, Bal the 2nd, chestnut mare got by Caradog, stands 15 hands high, grand action, perfectly sound, and a fast trotter. She and her offspring have won 16 Prizes at the Lampeter and district Shows. One of her offspring took the First Prize in Harness at Lampeter Show on the 7th of May, 1891, and the same day sold to Mr. Thomas Jones, Sutton, Salop, for £55. Bal the 2nd's dam, Bal the 1st, was got by Trotting Briton of Llechwedd-deri Uchaf, whose stock were nearly all very fast trotters. Bal the 1st was proved the fastest three-year-old filly of the season 1882, having beaten the winners of Cardigan and Carmarthenshire Races at Llanwnen, March 23rd.

WOODCOCK's g.-sire, Caradog, won 1st at Aberaeron and at Llanwrtyd in 1876, 1st at Newcastle Emlyn in 1877 and 1880. He is the sire of the wonderful trotter, Earl of Beaconsfield. Caradog's dam by Cardigan Comet 1st, winner of 21 First Prizes.

WOODCOCK's half-sister won 2 Firsts at Aberaeron last year as best Brood Mare and in Harness. His half-brother won 2 Firsts at Lampeter in 1899. Also his stock have been very successful, having taken Prizes at Talybont, Lampeter, Llanwenog, Alltyrodyn Arms, Llandyssul, Pencader, Llandilo, Pontlliw, and Ammanford; most of them Firsts.

WOODCOCK won the 2nd at Alltyrodyn Arms Entire Horse Show in 1895, 2nd at Llanelly in 1896, 1st at Carmarthen in 1896, a Prize of £20 at Aberystwyth in 1897, 1st at Llandovery in 1898, 2nd at Carmarthen in 1899, Reserve for £30 at Aberystwyth, 2nd at Llanelly, and 2nd at Carmarthen in 1900.

All Mares tried will be charged for, and all Mares to be at owner's risk.

☞ The Groom will specify the times and places of attendance.

J. D. Lewis, Printer, Gomerian Press, Llandyssul.

The development of the Welsh Cob breed this century both in conformation and numbers can be assessed by describing the winners of the George Prince of Wales Cup at the Royal Welsh Shows (see Appendix 2.1).

During the years 1904 to 1914 the numbers of in-hand Welsh Cobs competing at the Royal Welsh show were consistently healthy at between forty and sixty, even though many of them were pure Hackneys registered in the Welsh Stud Book. With Hackneys barred in the twenties, numbers fell to between twenty and thirty and reached dangerously low figures of ten to twenty in the lean thirties. The situation was not too secure after the second war with twenty-six entries in 1947 and only twenty-nine in 1957 and it took another twenty years (1977) for numbers to reach three figures (106) but these doubled to 211 in 1982. The increase during the eighties was astronomical to 335 in 1987 and 412 in 1989, settling down at between 520 and 540 in the years between 1993 and 1997.

The judge at the 1910 Show was Mr J. R. Bache of the Stud Farm, Knighton who had previously judged there also in 1907. Mr Bache was Secretary of the WPCS from 1909 to 1928. His choice for the Prince of Wales Cup was Crotten Ddu who, as her name implies, was a black mare, foaled in 1904, bred by David Thomas, Pentredavis Farm, Llanarthney, and owned by Thomas Morgan of 39, Station Road, Llanelly. Crotten Ddu was sired by Heart of Welsh Flyer, a Welsh-enough sounding name though he was never registered and there does not seem to be any other of his progeny in the Welsh Stud Book. As far as we can trace, this was the only occasion at which she competed at the Welsh National Show which was held in the owner's home town of Llanelly, and Thomas Morgan, recipient of the supreme accolade in Welsh Cobland does not seem to have owned any other Welsh Cobs. In 1911 with Tom James, Myrtle Hill, judging it was a battle between two of the largest studs of the day in the form of the Llwyn Stud owned by J. Marshall Dugdale, Chairman of Council of the WPCS and Evan Jones of the Manoravon Stud, Vice-President of the WPCS for 1908–9. Winner in 1911 was Marshall Dugdale's chestnut mare Llwyn Flashlight II, foaled in 1906 and sired by Llwyn Idloes Flyer who was reserve for this trophy in 1913 when the age restriction was removed.

Evan Jones's exhibit which was reserve for the trophy in 1911 was Cerdina, an up-to-height dark bay mare, foaled in 1905 and sired by

Llwyn Flashlight II, foaled in 1906, 1911 winner of PoW Cup.

Llwyn Idloes Flyer (foaled in 1893) sire of Llwyn Flashlight II.

Cerdin Briton out of Flower by Cribin Flyer and g-dam Fanny by Caradog, pure Welsh breeding through and through. Cerdin Briton was foaled in 1986, bred by Evan Griffiths, Blaencerdinfach, Ffostrasol, sired by Young Briton out of Cerdin Bess by Caradog and g-dam Bess by Old Comet. Cerdin Briton was purchased by Evan Jones from his breeder and had sired twelve of the forty-four lots offered at the Annual Manoravon Sale held on 15 October 1913. The sale catalogue was very impressive with a few lots sired by Greylight who had been sold to

Australia for 1,000 guineas and some more sired by Lord Towyvale who had fetched 500 guineas in a previous sale. Despite newspaper reports the following day quoting many horse and pony notables as having attended the sale, such as Sir Gilbert Greenall, Warrington; Mr Depeaux, Paris; Mr Houston, Glasgow and Mr Harrison, Manchester, the prices realised were disappointing. Cerdina (lot 21) fetched only thirty-two guineas – surely the lowest price ever for a Reserve winner of the George Prince of Wales Cup and described in the Catalogue as 'quiet in all harness and farm gears, is very fast and has been driven by a lady'.

At Swansea in 1912 Evan Jones went one stage better and won the cup with his home-bred stallion Manoravon Flyer, foaled in 1907 and sired by Llanio Flyer out of Favourite by King Flyer, g-dam Paleface by Welsh Flyer III. Manoravon Flyer won a board of Agriculture premium to run until 23 January 1913 after which he was sold for a high figure to Theodore Simpson and Sons, Bromhope Villa, Aurora, Illinois, USA.

Reserve in 1912 was another home-bred stallion Gwyndy Eiddwen, foaled in 1907 and sired by Cymro Du out of Gwyndy Fan by Cardigan Flyer, g-dam Fanny by Vyrnwy Flyer. Gwyndy Eiddwen was bred by W. Arthur Pughe of Gwyndy, Llanfyllin who was a very successful breeder of ponies and Cobs from the last century up to his death in 1945, the year when he was President of the WPCS.

Manoravon Flyer had won the class for stallions between 13 hands 2 in and 14 hands 2 in and Gwyndy Eiddwen was second in the over 14 hands 2 in class to the pure Hackney Atwick Junior under judges Mr Roger Howells of Kille Farm, Crickhowell, and Mr Ben Davies of Tyclyd, Beulah, but they were joined for the judging of the George Prince of Wales Cup by Mr N. Bennett Owen of Gwernafon, Llanidloes, who placed Gwyndy Eiddwen reserve.

Evan Jones, having won the cup in 1912 was appointed judge in 1913, accompanied by the Reverend John Owen, Taihirion, Tregaron, who was previously the owner of the Welsh Cob stallion Cardigan Briton, known throughout Welsh-speaking Wales as 'Pregethwr' – The Preacher. Mr Owen would attract large congregations to his chapel services, sometimes more to admire his mount than to listen to his sermons. Rumour had it that while the reverend gentleman was safely occupied in his pulpit, local farm lads would borrow his stallions to cover mares or hold races against the best Cobs of that area.

It was in 1913 that the nineteen-year-old King Flyer first won the Prince of Wales Cup for his owners Messrs H. M. and H. W. Jones of Mathrafal, a feat which he repeated in 1914. The influence of King Flyer on the breed will become apparent in the post-first war period when his son, Mathrafal Eiddwen won this trophy four times and daughter Polly of Pant won the mare class in 1925 and 1927.

Reserve for the Prince of Wales Cup in 1913 was Marshall Dugdale's Llwyn Idloes Flyer whom we have already met as the sire of the 1911 winner, Llwyn Flashlight II. Llywn Idloes Flyer had won the under 14 hands 2 in class, the second and third prizewinners to King Flyer in the over 14 hands 2 in class being two other exhibits from Marshall Dugdale's Stud: Llwyn Nigger and Llwyn Gambler sired by the 1909 winner High Stepping Gambler II. The 1912 judge Mr Bennett Owen was joined by the young Tom Jones Evans, son of the Welsh Cob historian Dafydd Evans to judge in 1914 with King Flyer winning from Evan Jones's aged mare Ping by Odwyn Comet and William Davies, Blaenpennal's winner of the smaller stallion class, Trotting Jack.

The photograph of King Flyer was the one used in breed pamphlets for the next thirty years or so; it shows excellent clean limbs without the coarse feather of so many of his contemporaries, especially the ones with Shire blood in their veins. From this photograph, King Flyer was shown also to possess a short, strong back and a good slope of shoulder with his wither way behind the vertical of his front legs. A present-day champion would be expected to have a sweeter head, but this is one of the easiest faults to correct.

The outbreak of war in 1914 prevented the holding of the Annual Show and there did not seem to be any enthusiasm to get the 'show on the road' again until the WPCS bravely stepped into the breach and it was Tom Jones Evans of Llwyncadfor who single-handedly at the WPCS AGM on 7 September 1920 stated that he was going to approach Mr David Davies of Llandinam, which he did and Mr Davies straight-away sent round the fiery cross, making it feasible to hold a 1922 Show at Wrexham.

By 1922 the Welsh Cob breed had become standardised and the Stud Book closed to outside blood for long enough to prevent Hackneys masquerading as Welsh Cobs. However, numbers were not plentiful, the entries at the 1922 Royal Welsh Show being six Welsh Cob stallions over 14 hands 2 in (section D of the Welsh Stud Book), five stallions under 14

King Flyer (foaled in 1894) winner of the PoW Cup in 1913 and 1914.

hands 2 in (section C), seven mares and only two in the youngstock class (both yearling fillies). Mr Meyrick Jones won the first class with Mathrafal Eiddwen an eight-year-old son of King Flyer from Major Dugdale's Llwyn Coming King, another son of the same King Flyer. Tom Jones Evans, who had moved from Llwyncadfor the previous year to become a tenant on the estate of Mrs Greene of the famous Grove Welsh Mountain Pony Stud won class 2 with his chestnut seven-year-old Llwynog Flyer which had been bred by Thomas Jones, Troedrhiwrhwch near Llwyncadfor. Second prize in this class went to David Rees's Mathrafal Brenin. Pontfaen Lady Model who won the mare class was only five years old and the youngest in the class, bred and owned by Thomas Davies of Llechwedd and Pontfaen farms, Lampeter. Lady Model was sired by Welsh Model, owned by one of the best-known stallion owners of those days, Richard Morgan, Lluestybroga, Llangeitho. Welsh Model was g-sire of the influential Cardi Llwyd who, in turn was g-sire of Llanarth Braint. Welsh Model's background is Welsh through and through: sired by Caradog Flyer by young Caradog by Caradog by Welsh Jack by Cymro Llwyd he goes back to the beginning of recorded pedigrees.

Welsh Model had been second to Llwyn Idloes Flyer at the 1913 Royal Welsh Show and second also the following year to Trotting Jack. Pontfaen Lady Model's dam was Lady Gwenog III, bred by Thomas Davies in 1906, sired by the 15-hand Llwyncadfor Hackney stallion Dilham Confidence (chapter 1) out of the roan Lady Gwenog by the famous mountain pony stallion, Dyoll Starlight. Lady Model won the George Prince of Wales Cup and, since Tom Jones Evans now resided in England, Llwynog Flyer could not compete for this award and David Rees's Mathrafal Brenin beat Meyrick Jones's Mathrafal Eiddwen for the reserve position.

Pontfaen Lady Model won the cup for the second time the following year after winning the mare class of 14 entries from Major Dugdale's Hwylog Peggy, a daughter of Trotting Jack. The Agricultural Gazette photograph which I have of Lady Model shows my father holding the foal. The two Cob stallion classes were amalgamated, Tom Jones Evans winning again with Llwynog Flyer from Meyrick Jones's Mathrafal Eiddwen and Richard Morgan's Welsh Model. By 1924, Pontfaen Lady Model had been sold to Mrs Lyell of Neston, Cheshire, who had a very

Welsh Model (foaled in 1910) sire of Pontfaen Lady Model, 1922 recipient of the PoW Cup.

formidable showing string of Welsh mountain pony mares, but Lady Model could stand no higher than fifth in a twelve-strong class won by Evan and Harry Evans's Wyre Lady by Ceitho Welsh Comet, Major Dugdale's Hwylog Peggy and Daniel Williams's Graig Fly.

Pontfaen Lady Model's recent claim to fame is as the g-dam of Hendy Brenin (foaled in 1944) a much sought-after sire for example, he sired the 1980 Royal Welsh female champion Porthvaynor Gold Dust, and was g-sire of the 1983 and 1984 Prince of Wales Cup winner, Derwen Princess. By 1930, after producing Craven Llwynog's Model (youngstock champion at the 1927 Royal Welsh Show) and Craven Cymro (winner of the Prince of Wales Cup in 1934) in 1927 for Mr Tom Jones Evans, he sold her to his brother Robert Evans, Dolgian, Newcastle Emlyn (quite near to their birthplace, Llwyncadfor) who in 1935 bred Lady Welsh Flyer by Myrtle Welsh Flyer (Prince of Wales Cup winner in 1933 and 1939) out of Ponfaen Lady Model. Lady Welsh Flyer was sold to William Thomas, Fronwen, Llandysul for whom she bred Hendy Brenin in 1944 sired by Meiarth Royal Eiddwen.

Pontfaen Lady Model, 1922 recipient of the PoW Cup, also won it in 1923.

The 1924 stallion class was won by David Rees's Mathrafal Brenin from John Richards's Llethi Valiant (a son of Ceitho Welsh Comet) and Mathrafal Brenin went a stage further to win the championship from Wyre Lady and Hwylog Peggy. Llethi Valiant emerges later to win the cup in 1931 and be sire of the four-times champion Meiarth Welsh Maid and g-sire of the 1955 champion Teifi Welsh Maid.

Llwynog Flyer, winner of the stallion class at the 1922 RW Show.

Wyre Lady was regarded by many of the leading judges of the time to be 'one of the choicest in living memory' but did not leave any mark on the breed. Her daughter Wyre Queen was placed in the youngstock class at the 1924 Royal Welsh Show and, along with Llethi Valiant and a two-year-old colt Eiddwen Welsh Flyer by Ceitho Welsh Comet won the 'county' competition for

Cardiganshire for the best group of Welsh Cobs. Wyre Lady was sold at a horse sale in England in 1929 and was never heard of again.

In 1925 with Mr T. H. Vaughan of Sychtyn judging, Mathrafal Brenin notched up his second Prince of Wales Cup triumph, the trophy being presented to him by Lord Noel Buxton the first Labour Minister of Agriculture. This was Mathrafal Brenin's last Royal Welsh Show appearance and he died suddenly of anthrax while travelling through Breconshire in 1928. Mathrafal Brenin, though small in inches, proved to be a great progenitor, ancestor of the following Royal Welsh Show Cob champions: Brenin Gwalia, Mathrafal, Llwynog-y-Garth, Rhystyd Prince, Honyton Michael ap Braint, Llanarth Brummell, Parc Lady, Meiarth Welsh Maid, Tyhen Mattie, Geler Daisy, Llanarth Flying Comet and many later champions. The winning mare in 1925 was J. Davies and Son's nineteen-year-old Polly of Pant who returned two years later to win it again, on both occasions with Hwylog Peggy second, Peggy having also been second in 1923 and 1924! We shall meet Polly of Pant later as g-dam of the 1928 champion Pant Grey Star.

Polly of Pant (foaled in 1906), winner of the mare class in 1925 and 1927. G-dam of Pant Grey Star, winner of the PoW Cup in 1928. Photo by W H Bustin.

In 1926 with Mathrafal Brenin having retired from competition, the championship went to Mathrafal Eiddwen whom we have already met as the son of the 1913 and 1914 champion King Flyer. Mathrafal Eiddwen was foaled in 1914 and had already won the Royal Welsh stallion class in 1922 and in 1926 to win the class had to beat the 1931 champion Llethi Valiant and the 1933 and 1939 champion Myrtle Welsh Flyer. Hwylog Peggy had been bought by John Jones and Son of Dinarth Hall from Marshall Dugdale and won the mare class and was reserve for the championship. In those days judges were allowed to judge animals which they had bred or owned and Hwylog Peggy was second to Polly of Pant in 1927 with Major Marshall Dugdale judging; the championship going for the second time to Mathrafal Eiddwen who had won his class again from Myrtle Welsh Flyer. The entries in the four classes were up to thirty-two and were given a good boost when representatives of the Spanish Government bought several stallions and colts including Brenin Cymru (by Mathrafal Brenin) from my grandfather.

Mathrafal Eiddwen is one of only three Welsh Cobs (the others being Meiarth Welsh Maid and Parc Lady) to have won the George Prince of Wales Cup four times; he would have made even greater history had he won it in 1928 but judge Mr Edgar Herbert placed Mathrafal Eiddwen second in his class to Llethi Valiant and later awarded the championship to the winning mare Pant Grey Star. There are many Cob enthusiasts today who can still remember Pant Grey Star on account of her spectacular movement; her dam was an unregistered mare named 'Bess', surprisingly bred by an unregistered sire out of the 1925 and 1927 winning mare, Polly of Pant. The championship of the Welsh Pony of Cob-type section at this Show was won by my father's Seren Ceulan and when I was born (some years later!) judge Mr Edgar Herbert was appointed my god-father!

In 1929 the judge was Mr J. R. Bache who had given up the Secretaryship of the WPCS the previous year and had judged at the Royal Welsh previously in 1907, 1910 and 1922. The Welsh Cob section

Mathrafal Eiddwen, winner of the PoW Cup in 1927, 1928, 1929 and 1930. Photo by G H Parsons.

Llethi Valiant, 1931 recipient of the PoW Cup, pictured here at home and (BELOW) in the showring. Photo by G H Parsons.

was the strongest (ten stallions, seven mares, five three-year-olds and two two-year-olds) compared with thirty-two Welsh Mountain ponies in five classes and four classes of Welsh Ponies Cob-type with nine entries, the latter being the cause of so much concern that the new categorisation of section B to Welsh ponies of riding-type was put into force at the 1931 AGM of the WPCS. Cob stallions ended up in the following order: Mathrafal Eiddwen, Myrtle Welsh Flyer, Caerseddfan Stepping Flyer, Llwyn Dazzler, Llethi Valiant, Blaenwaun True Briton, Ffynonwen Young Defiance (g-g-sire of the 1957 Royal Welsh champion Princess), Windsor Druidstone, Capel Comet and St David Comet. Thomas Rees of Blaenwaun, placed only sixth with his Blaenwaun True Briton, received some recompense when he won the mare class with Blaenwaun Flora Temple from Pant Grey Star, Lan Carnation, Pistyll Nance, Llethi Flower (dam of Llethi Valiant), Dinam Megan and Pantlleinau Blodwen (g-dam of the exceptional sire Cahn Dafydd), in that order.

1930 was the last year for Mathrafal Eiddwen to compete and win the Prince of Wales Cup for the fourth time. The judge, Mr Tom Jenkins of Kilvrough, Gower (President of the WPCS 1939–44), writing the judge's report in the RWAS journal says 'The typical Welsh Cob Mathrafal Eiddwen won his class although he is getting to the end of his showyard career. He is a grand old horse and full of Welsh character. The second prizewinner Myrtle Welsh Flyer is a really good animal and was well shown but he is not quite as typical as the winner.' This show saw the appearance in the mare class under the ownership of John Jones and Son of Dinarth Hall, of the beautiful black mare Cwmcau Lady Jet, daughter of Trotting Jack. Cwmcau Lady Jet was bred by W. T. and O. M. Evans in 1919 in my home village and had won prizes at Talybont Shows since 1923 (my father winning the championships there in 1922, 1923 and 1924 with Seren Ceulan) and the WPCS medal at Llanrhystyd in 1925. In her class at the 1930 Royal Welsh Show were three other famous mares, Blaenwaun Flora Temple, Pantlleinau Blodwen and Pant Grey Star, standing in that order. Mathrafal Eiddwen stayed on at Mathrafal for a few years at stud alongside his son Mathrafal Broadcast (foaled in 1926); the latter's greatest claim to fame being as the g-sire of the post-war foundation sire of Section B: Criban Victor. Mathrafal Eiddwen was then sold to various Cardiganshire Studs ending up at Pentrebrain in 1937 where he died in 1940. His influence on the Welsh Cob breed during those three years at Pentrebrain was phenomenal. Mated to the 1935 Prince of Wales Cup winner, Dewi Black Bess, Mathrafal Eiddwen produced Eiddwen's Model (in 1939) and Eiddwen's Pride (in 1940). Eiddwen's Model was sold to Anglesey where she produced Gwalchmai Welsh Model (in 1953), later to become the foundation of a very successful bloodline at Menai Stud. Prior to this, Eiddwen's Model in 1950 produced Pentre Eiddwen's Model, dam of the 1962 Royal Welsh male champion Pentre Rainbow and in 1951 produced Pentre Eiddwen's Pearl dam of the 1963 and 1965 champion Pentre Eiddwen's Doll. Eiddwen's Pride produced Pentre Eiddwen Flyer, sire of Pentre Eiddwen's Pearl and Brenin-y-Bryniau. But the greatest influence of Mathrafal Eiddwen of course came via the great Pentre Eiddwen Comet (foaled in 1946), sired by Eiddwen's Image (Mathrafal Eiddwen x Dewi Rosina, daughter of Dewi Black Bess) out of his own g-dam: Dewi Black Bess. Apart from winning six Royal Welsh championships himself Pentre Eiddwen Comet sired the other Royal Welsh champions Geler Daisy, Tyhen Comet, Nebo Black Magic and Llanarth Flying Comet as well as being g-sire of Pentre Rainbow, Derwen Rosina, Rhystyd Prince, Parc Rachel, Geler Neli, Derwen Rosinda and Derwen Princess. It is well

Dewi Black Bess (foaled in 1926) winner of the PoW Cup in 1935, dam of Dewi Rosina winner of the PoW Cup in 1953, also dam of Pentre Eiddwen Comet winner of the PoW Cup in 1951 and 1956. Photo by G H Parsons.

nigh impossible these days to find a respectable Welsh Cob without some Pentre Eiddwen Comet blood flowing in its veins.

By having Mr T. J. Jones of Dinarth Hall judging in 1931, the section was robbed of some of its most successful exhibits; however, entries kept up fairly well with eight stallions, four mares and four in the youngstock class. The stallion class was full of talent ending up in the order: Craven Cymro, Llethi Valiant, Mathrafal Plunder, Mathrafal Broadcast, Comet Bach, Paith Flyer II (sire of Pistyll Goldflake and Victory Maid, dam of Princess), Gwalia Victor (sire of Brenin Gwalia) and Cystanog Trotting Comet. The mares were Pantlleinau Blodwen, Lan Carnation, Rhystyd Sunrise (dam of Rhystyd Trustee, sire of Rhystyd Titbit, g-g-dam of Royal Welsh champions Rhystyd Prince and Rhystyd Meredith) and Ormond Jolly (g-g-dam of four-times champion Parc Lady).

Judge Thomas John Jones (President of the WPCS in 1928–9) writing in the *Royal Welsh Society Journal* said that 'Craven Cymro was a clear leader, being well shown, outstanding in conformation and giving a nice, though not extravagant, display. Llethi Valiant who was second is a real Welshman with abundance of courage, but shown rather light and lacking the conformation of the winner when pulled up.' Craven Cymro was champion and Llethi Valiant was reserve, but since Craven Cymro was bred and owned by Tom Jones Evans of Craven Arms, the Prince of Wales Cup went to Llethi Valiant. Thus Llethi Valiant who had competed valiantly for this trophy since 1924 and won his class in 1928, eventually had his name engraved on the trophy at his last Royal Welsh appearance, though sadly only by default. Craven Cymro so impressed judge Mr Jones that he bought him. Incidentally, he was also so impressed with his champion pony of Cob-type, my father's Ceulan Comet, that he bought him also and exported him to Australia two years later. Craven Cymro in the ownership of Dinarth Hall was awarded the Prince of Wales Cup at the 1934 Royal Welsh Show, the fact that he had been bred in Shropshire presumably having been overlooked.

Craven Cymro's dam was the 1922 and 1923 champion Pontfaen Lady Model, sold to Allan Lyell (President of the WPCS in 1927–8) in 1924; she was bought by Tom Jones Evans in 1925 with a colt foal by Llwynog Flyer at foot. This foal, named Craven Llwynog's Model, was youngstock champion at the 1927 Royal Welsh Show and was sold for export there.

By 1932 Welsh Cob numbers had reached a dangerously low level (though in the 1936 *Journal* Captain Howson writes that things had gone 'from bad to worse') with four stallions, eight mares (of which two had no particulars of name or breeding) and two youngstock. Judge Meyrick

Craven Cymro, winner of the PoW Cup in 1934.

Jones of Mathrafal placed the local stallion, Caerseddfan Stepping Flyer, above the previous winner, Craven Cymro, Paith Flyer II and Mab-y-Brenin (sire of the great Mathrafal which Mr Threadgold of Welshpool had bought from my grandfather earlier that year). Caerseddfan Stepping Flyer was awarded the Prince of Wales Cup from Dinarth Hall's Cwmcae Lady Jet who had won her class from Pantlleinau Blodwen, Rheidol Trotting Girl, Cwmsevin Nancy and Maylord Wonder. It is not generally realised that the Maylord Stud has been breeding Welsh Cobs for seventy years. One of the top sires of recent years, Oakhatch Cymydog Da (foaled in 1972), is out of Maylord Charm (f. 1963) out of Maylord Pride (f. 1958) out of Maylord Fair Lady (f. 1955) out of Maylord Lady Model (f. 1932) out of Maylord Wonder (foaled in 1925 and exhibited at the 1932 Royal Welsh Show).

Caerseddfan Stepping Flyer had been purchased by the Maylord Stud one week before the Show but it is the name of the former owner George Gittins which is engraved on the trophy. Captain Howson describes Caerseddfan Stepping Flyer as a 'picturesque red chestnut with bone and dashing action'. Captain Howson, bemoaning the total number of twelve Welsh Cobs at Llandrindod and blaming the withdrawal of War Office and Treasury Premium grants, continues 'In spite of the growth of other means of locomotion, there remain many uses for strong, spanking,

Caerseddfan Stepping Flyer, 1932 winner of PoW Cup. Shown for owners by Mr Granville Mathias. Photo by G H Parsons.

lion-hearted Cobs, both in and out of Wales and it is sincerely to be hoped that those who own good breeding stock of the true and tested lines of blood will hold on until the dawn of those better times which optimists believe will come again.' Captain Howson's vision was truly justified by the 536 in-hand Welsh Cobs entered for the 1997 Royal Welsh Show.

In 1933 the Show was held where it all began, at Aberystwyth in the heart of Cardiganshire cob-land and they made a very brave display with seven stallions, thirteen mares and four youngsters (the top two were disqualified for being over-age!). The stallions in order were Myrtle Welsh Flyer (now aged sixteen years), Craven Cymro (owned by Dinarth Hall), Paith Flyer II, Llanedy Trustful Gambler, last year's champion Caerseddfan Stepping Flyer, Rhystyd Trustee and Brechfa Welsh Flyer. Cwmcae Lady Jet repeated her mare class triumph from Pant Grey Star (who judge Matthew Williams described in his report as 'better looking on parade than when standing', Brombil Fly, Rheidol Trotting Girl, Dewi Black Bess and Sian Gwalia, owned by my grandfather. Pontfaen Lady Model was shown in the ownership of Mr A. Lashford of Birmingham but her age was against her.

Numbers at Llandudno in 1934 were disappointing, with Dinarth Hall (which was within a short walking distance of the show site) winning both Welsh Cob and Welsh pony of Cob-type classes and the two championships and the two reserves! Craven Cymro won the championship and the Prince of Wales Cup despite not having been bred in Wales, but if he had been disqualified for his birthplace, the cup would have gone to Dinarth Hall anyway, with the winning mare Cwmcau Lady Jet who won from Sian Gwalia, Dewi Black Bess, Hwylog Peggy and Daisy Belle, in that order.

If Welsh Cob entries in 1934 were poor, in 1935 the situation was desperate, with only three stallions, five mares and four youngsters. Myrtle Welsh Flyer again won the stallion class but was moved down a peg for the championship which was won by Mr J. O. Davies's Dewi Black Bess (though the cup itself is incorrectly engraved as having been won by Dewi Princess) who won her class from Cwmcau Lady Jet, Teifi of Hercws, Sian Gwalia and Morfa Marina. The youngstock winner was Dewi Princess (daughter of Dewi Black Bess) from Nan Gwalia (owned by my cousin Billy Evans whose daughter continues breeding under the Frongoch prefix). This dire situation was fortunately not always in evidence at all Welsh Shows: at Lampeter Show that year there were over fifty entries in five classes and Sian Gwalia was champion, beating Dewi Black Bess and Teifi of Hercws, her Royal Welsh vanquishers.

Captain Howson records Welsh Cob entries at the 1936 Show as having gone 'from bad to worse'; Mr T. J. Jones of Dinarth Hall was the judge, thereby depriving the entries of their most loyal supporter. Myrtle Welsh Flyer beat two rather 'middle of the road' exhibits to win the male championship easily despite his nineteen years. The females had things all their own way for the Prince of Wales Cup which went to J. D. Evans's ten-year-old Teify of Hercws, daughter of Ceitho Welsh Comet from Sian Gwalia and I am the proud possessor of the reserve card for the 1936 Prince of Wales Cup, something which I value greatly, despite the fact that there were only ten entries in the entire section. This was the last show for Sian Gwalia, who died suddenly shortly afterwards.

Sian Gwalia, reserve for the PoW Cup in 1934 and 1936. Owned by Mr L O Williams (Wynne Davies's grandfather). Shown by Mr E S Davies (father of Wynne Davies). Photo by G H Parsons.

Owing to lack of support, at the 1937 Royal Welsh Show the Welsh Cob youngstock class was dropped and only two mares and four stallions made up the entire section. Teify of Hercws won the Prince of Wales Cup for the second time from the winning stallion, Cystanog Trotting Comet, a stallion described by Captain Howson as 'boasting an intelligent and true cob head endowed with small prick ears, a pleasing outlook and a wealthy middlepiece but his action left something to be wished for'. The Show deserved more support from Cob breeders since the second and third prize stallions, Mathrafal Broadcast and Welsh Rebound, were sold for export to the United States and Australia respectively.

Since the 1938 Show at Cardiff was a combined Show with the visit of the Royal Agricultural Society of England the trophies were not awarded; Parc Stud's Parc Express was the only exhibit in the stallion class and was reserve for the male championship to Mr Meyrick Jones's two-year-old colt Mathrafal. Teify of Hercws, Dewi Black Bess, Pistyll Nance and Lady Gwenog 6th ended up in that order after a great battle between the top two mares, both from the Tregaron area, both twelve years old and both sired by Ceitho Welsh Comet who was, by then, dead. Black Bess was pulled in first by the judge Captain Howson, who described her as 'quality all through' but was a little listless on the day and gave way to Teify of Hercws, who gave a very dashing show which she kept up to the end. Mr Matthew Williams judged at the 1939 Show and awarded the Prince of Wales Cup (as he had previously done in 1933) to Mr Tom James's Myrtle Welsh Flyer; Captain Howson describing the twenty-one-year-old stallion and the elderly owner as 'both having found the secret of perpetual youth'. There were still only two classes, Mr Wood-Jones's Cymro'r Wy who stood second to Myrtle Welsh Flyer was reserve for the Prince of Wales Cup from the winning mare (from a class of three) Messrs David Lloyd and Son's Meiarth Pride. There were no Royal Welsh Shows held during the second World War years 1940–6 nor during 1948, due to petrol rationing. Most of the champions since 1947 are featured in the stud chapters in this volume.

Appendix 2.1 Royal Welsh Show Prince of Wales Cup winners (Champion Welsh Cob)

date	where held	winner	judge
1908	Aberystwyth	Pride of the Hills (H. P. Edwards)	Sir R. Green Price
1909	Aberystwyth	High Stepping Gambler II (E. Davies)	John Hill
1910	Llanelly	Croten Ddu (Thomas Morgan)	J. R. Bache
1911	Welshpool	Llwyn Flashlight II (Marshall Dugdale)	Tom James
1912	Swansea	Manorafon Flyer (Evan Jones)	R. Howells, B. Davies, N. Bennett Owen
1913	Portmadoc	King Flyer (Meyrick Jones, Mathrafal)	Evan Jones, Rev. John Owen
1914	Newport	King Flyer (Meyrick Jones, Mathrafal)	N. Bennett Owen, T. Jones Evans
1922	Wrexham	Pontfaen Lady Model (Thomas Davies)	J. R. Bache
1923	Welshpool	Pontfaen Lady Model (Thomas Davies)	Tom James
1924	Bridgend	Mathrafal Brenin (D. Rees, Penuwch)	W. Arthur Pughe
1925	Carmarthen	Mathrafal Brenin (D. Rees, Penuwch)	T. H. Vaughan
1926	Bangor	Mathrafal Eiddwen (Meyrick Jones)	T. Jones Evans
1927	Swansea	Mathrafal Eiddwen (Meyrick Jones)	Major Dugdale
1928	Wrexham	Pant Grey Star (J. Davies)	Edgar Herbert
1929	Cardiff	Mathrafal Eiddwen (Meyrick Jones)	J. R. Bache
1930	Caernarfon	Mathrafal Eiddwen (Meyrick Jones)	T. E. Jenkins
1931	Llanelly	Llethi Valiant (J. Richards)	T. J. Jones
1932	Llandrindod	Caerseddfan Stepping Flyer (G. Gittins)	Meyrick Jones
1933	Aberystwyth	Myrtle Welsh Flyer (Tom James)	Matthew Williams
1934	Llandudno	Craven Cymro (J. Jones & Son, Dinarth Hall)	T. J. Mathias
1935	Haverfordwest	Dewi Black Bess (J. O. Davies)	T. E. Jenkins
1936	Abergele	Teifi of Hercws (J. D. Evans)	T. J. Jones
1937	Monmouth	Teifi of Hercws (J. D. Evans)	T. Jones Evans
1938	Cardiff	(not offered: RASE)	
1939	Caernarfon	Myrtle Welsh Flyer (Tom James)	Matthew Williams

Appendix 2.1 continues

date	where held	winner	judge
1947	Carmarthen	Meiarth Welsh Maid (David Lloyd)	J. Morgan Evans
1948	(no Show)		
1949	Swansea	Meiarth Welsh Maid (David Lloyd)	Captain T. A. Howson
1950	Abergele	Meiarth Welsh Maid (David Lloyd)	J. M. Harvard
1951	Llanelwedd	Pentre Eiddwen Comet (John Hughes)	D. O. Morgan
1952	Caernarfon	Mathrafal (E. D. Richards)	Gwilym Morris
1953	Cardiff	Dewi Rosina (E. Roscoe Lloyd)	A. L. Williams
1954	Machynlleth	Meiarth Welsh Maid (David Lloyd)	Douglas Meredith
1955	Haverfordwest	Teifi Welsh Maid (J. H. Davies)	J. Edwards
1956	Rhyl	Pentre Eiddwen Comet (John Hughes)	J. O. Davies
1957	Aberystwyth	Princess (T. B. J. Evans)	I. Osborne Jones
1958	Bangor	Parc Lady (D. O. Morgan)	T. J. Thomas
1959	Margam	Parc Lady (D. O. Morgan)	J. Berry
1960	Welshpool	Parc Lady (D. O. Morgan)	Mrs I. M. Yeomans
1961	Llandeilo	Parc Lady (D. O. Morgan)	D. Edwardes
1962	Wrexham	Tyhen Mattie (W. L. Lloyd Davies)	H. Ll. Richards
1963	Llanelwedd	Tyngwndwn Cream Boy (E. Price)	E. Evans
1964	Llanelwedd	Llanarth Brummel (Miss Ann Wheatcroft)	E. G. E. Griffith
1965	Llanelwedd	Pentre Eiddwen Comet (John Hughes)	J. M. Havard
1966	Llanelwedd	Derwen Rosina (E. Roscoe Lloyd)	J. F. Lewis
1967	Llanelwedd	Derwen Rosina (reserve Champion awarded Cup)	
		Honyton Michael ap Braint (champion) not bred in Wales	Miss Wheatcroft
1968	Llanelwedd	Derwen Rosina (E. Roscoe Lloyd)	J. H. Davies
1969	Llanelwedd	Tyhen Comet (John Hughes)	W. Jones
1970	Llanelwedd	Brenin Dafydd (Jones Brothers, Fronarth Stud)	S. D. Morgan
1971	Llanelwedd	Parc Rachel (S. D. Morgan & Sons)	J. Lloyd
1972	Llanelwedd	Parc Rachel (S. D. Morgan & Sons)	Mostyn Isaac
1973	Llanelwedd	Nebo Black Magic (E. Roscoe Lloyd & Son)	Miss P. Taylor
1974	Llanelwedd	Llanarth Flying Comet (Miss Pauline Taylor)	I. J. R. Lloyd
1975	Llanelwedd	Parc Rachel (S. D. Morgan & Sons)	T. J. Gwyn Price

date	where held	winner	judge
1976	Llanelwedd	Llanarth Flying Comet (Llanarth Stud & Farms)	J. Gareth Evans
1977	Llanelwedd	Llanarth Flying Comet (Llanarth Stud & Farms)	Mrs C. Richards
1978	Llanelwedd	Llanarth Flying Comet (Llanarth Stud & Farms)	A. L. Williams
1979	Llanelwedd	Ffoslas Black Lady (Mr & Mrs W. J. Evans)	Ieu James
1980	Llanelwedd	Ffoslas Flying Rocket (Miss Heulwen Haf Jones)	J. R. Rees, BA
1981	Llanelwedd	Derwen Rosinda (E. Roscoe Lloyd & Son)	W. Geraint Jones
1982	Llanelwedd	Cyttir Telynor (Jones Brothers, Fronarth Stud)	T. B. J. Evans
1983	Llanelwedd	Derwen Princess (E. Roscoe Lloyd & Son)	W. E. Rowlands
1984	Llanelwedd	Derwen Princess (E. Roscoe Lloyd & Son)	D. R. Higgins
1985	Llanelwedd	Derwen Viscountess (Mr & Mrs D. J. Haak)	W. L. Harris
1986	Llanelwedd	Derwen Groten Goch (Mr & Mrs I. J. R. Lloyd & Son)	G. E. Evans
1987	Llanelwedd	Cyttir Telynor (Jones Brothers & Gwyn Jones)	T. J. Gwyn Price
1988	Llanelwedd	Nebo Daniel (Mr & Mrs W. G. Jones)	Mrs Alison Mountain
1989	Llanelwedd	Derwen Dameg (Mr & Mrs I. J. R. Lloyd & Son)	J. E. Jones
1990	Llanelwedd	Derwen Groten Goch (Mr & Mrs I. J. R. Lloyd & Son)	I. J. Phillips
1991	Llanelwedd	Pantanamlwg Red Fox (E. J. Evans)	Daff Davies
1992	Llanelwedd	Derwen Groten Goch (Mr & Mrs I. J. R. Lloyd & Son)	D. J. Jones
1993	Llanelwedd	Horeb Euros (Mr & Mrs R. Rees)	Mrs P. E. Vestey
1994	Llanelwedd	Nebo Hywel (Mr & Mrs W. G. Jones)	Mrs G. M. Dale
1995	Llanelwedd	Gellifach ap Dafydd (E. W. O. Davies)	Miss R. Philipson-Stow
1996	Llanelwedd	Fronarth Welsh Model (Jones Brothers and Mr & Mrs Gwyu Jones)	W. Lloyd
1997	Llanewedd	Trevallion Giorgio (Nelson Smith)	L. Bigley
1998	Llanewedd	Ebbw Victor (D. R. Weeks)	Mrs Mary Edwards

CHAPTER THREE

Welsh Cob premium stallions

OWNING STALLIONS FOR service had been a practice in Wales since before recorded history; one stallion is known to have been taken around Montgomeryshire farms in the thirteenth century. The livelihood of many large families living on smallholdings in mid-Wales revolved around the success or otherwise of a Stud stallion. The most popular stallions would have free food and stabling as they travelled around the farms, while only a few farmers offered stabling, even with payment, to second-rate horses. A verse relating to hard times experienced by owners of mediocre stallions went:

> Dwy geiniog mewn cyfyngder
> A ges gan Ianto Tinker
> Gwell yw trêd yr ambarel
> Na dilyn cel Ty Tyler

> When I was financially in distress
> I received two pence from Ianto the Tinker
> There is a better trade in umbrellas
> Than in travelling the Ty Tyler stallion.

There are cases of children brought up in large families dependent on their father's income from service fees, who later became famous in the history of Wales. One such case was Dr Thomas Jones, CH, LLD, Parliamentary Private Secretary to Lloyd George and until his death in 1955, President of the University College of Wales at Aberystwyth. Dr

Thomas Jones writing about his childhood in 'Rhymney Memories' writes that his grandfather was Benjamin Jones of Gwynfil, a very small 'croft' in Llangeitho; Benjamin Jones travelled Cardigan Comet around Wales and as far as Hereford and Gloucester, the animal proudly wearing a leather collar adorned with fourteen brass shields engraved with his showring successes: Aberaeron 1861, 1864, 1865, 1866, 1870; Aberystwyth 1861; Carmarthen 1868, 1870, 1871, 1872; Cardigan 1864, 1865, 1866 and 1870. Thomas Jones's son, Tristan Jones (brother of politician Baroness White) bought the colt foal, Ceulan Gwynfil Comet (Llangybi Seldom Seen x Meiarth Modern Maid), from us at the 1966 Llanarth Sale having traced his pedigree back via several channels to Cardigan Comet (foaled in 1860).

The three Rees brothers (chapter 7) travelled their stallions for over sixty years; Llwyncadfor would have ten or more stallions, many of which would travel, similarly Tom James, Myrtle Hill, and they would advertise their stallions in glowing terms on their stud cards. My grandfather, L. O. Williams, had stud cards with six stallions advertised but, I believe, standing at stud at home.

When one considers the many thousands of working 'Cobs' which were in the Principality at the turn of the century, indeed thousands were sold annually to the dairy and newspaper trades in the English towns, the numbers of the better animals which were registered in the Welsh Stud Book were minimal. Only 114 section C (Cob stallions from 13.2hh to 14.2hh) and 94 section D (over 14.2hh) in total were registered in the first ten volumes of the Welsh Stud Book, covering the years 1902 to 1911 with many of these foaled in pre-Stud Book times e.g. Eiddwen Flyer foaled in 1877 and registered in volume 10 (1911). A good third of these 208 stallions were pure Hackneys without a drop of Welsh blood in their veins and only registered in the Welsh Stud Book so that they could compete at Welsh Shows and win WPCS medals.

The Royal Commission on Horse Breeding held in 1888 was informed that premiums awarded to stallions would encourage owners to keep a better standard of stallion rather than the 'cheapest' stallion and these could be offered to tenant farmers at a maximum fee of 50s each. The Queen's Premiums were introduced in 1888; these became the King's Premiums in 1901 and in 1911 – the awarding Body was the Board of Agriculture and Fisheries. The Commons Act was passed in 1908 and the Church Stretton Pony Society was awarding premiums for

Welsh Mountain Pony stallions to run out on the hills. In 1912 the Board of Agriculture and Fisheries extended the award of premiums to pony and Cob stallions standing for public service; five premiums were awarded to Welsh Cobs, four to Welsh Mountain ponies, six to Fells and six to New Forest stallions – a total of twenty-one.

Regulations and conditions of award of Board's Premiums to Welsh Cob stallions

1. The average value of a Board's Premium to a Welsh Cob Stallion is £50, paid by the Board as follows:

	£	s	d
Premium of £20 paid at the time of award ...	20	0	0
Service Fee of £1 1s a mare for 25 mares, to which free nominations have been awarded by a County Committee paid after the close of the Service Season	26	5	0
Foal Fee of 5/- a foal (average number 15) paid after the close of the Foaling Season ...	3	15	0
	£50	0	0

2. The Board are prepared to award, on the recommendation of County Committees, a limited number of Premiums to Stallions of the Old Welsh stamp, 14 hands or over, and not over twenty years of age.

County Committees had to be set up to regulate the allocation of premiums, to advertise the routes undertaken by the premium stallions and to select twenty-five mares of the Old Welsh stamp to which they could allocate free services, the only payment for the owner of the mare being the 2/6 groom's fee. The Board of Agriculture paid the veterinary cost of certifying that the stallion was sound, suitable for breeding purpose and free from diseases and defects: cataract, roaring, whistling, ringbone, sidebone, navicular disease, shivering, stringhalt and defective genital organs.

List of Welsh Cob stallions to which Premiums were awarded by the Board in 1912

Name of stallion	Name of owner	Address of owner	County in which located
Beaconsfield Flyer (532)	J. R. Bache	Stud Farm Knighton	Radnorshire
Briton Flyer (622)	David Davies	Blaenpistyll Farm	Cardiganshire
Comet Bach (533)	Sir Edward J. Webley-Parry Pryse, Bart.	Gogerddan, Bow Street	Cardiganshire
Gwrda Welsh Boy	Morgan Evans	Wern, Llanwrda, Carmarthenshire	Carmarthenshire
King Flyer (35)	H. M. and H. W. Jones	Mathyrafal, Meifod, Welshpool	Montgomeryshire
Llwyn Planet (523)	J. M. Dugdale	Llwyn, Llanfyllin, Mont.	Montgomeryshire

Comet Bach (foaled in 1891) one of two premium stallions for Cardiganshire in 1912.

The names of the twenty-five mares which were selected by the Local Committee for free services were printed in the Welsh Stud Book.

1912 List of free nomination mares

Name of stallion

Llwyn Planet (523).

Name of Mare	Description	Name and address of owner of mare
4283 Lucy of Penyfford	Black, 13-3	D. Evans, Penyfford, Llanfihangel, Llanfyllin.
4295 Pollie of Maesclynog	Chest., 14-2	E. Lloyd, Maesclynog, Llanerfyl, Welshpool.
4300 Polly of Llangedwin	Chest., 14-1	E. Roberts, Bridge Inn, Llangedwin, Oswestry.
4310 Shill	Chest., 14-1	W. Ellis, Bradford House, Llanfyllin.
4296 Polly of Caerfach	Brown, 14-0	J. D. Edwards, Caerfach, Llansilin.
4344 Punch	Chest., 15-0	Ellis Gittins, Brynadda, Llanwddyn, Oswestry.
4224 Polly of Pantyffynon	Red ro., 13-1	W. Evans, Pantyffynon, Llanwddyn, Oswestry.
4236 Bessie of Aber	Brown, 14-2	E. Lloyd, Abermarchant, Llanwddyn, Oswestry.
4244 Black Bess	Black, 14-1	D. Davies, Maes Maengwynedd, Llanrhaidr, Oswentry.
4259 Dentyn Blue	Bay, 13-3	W. D. Hughes, New Mills, Llanrhaidr.
4346 Tyisa Violet	Brown, 14-3	W. Morris, Tyisa, Maengwynedd, Llanrhaidr, Oswestry.
4233 Berwyn Dolly	Chest., 14-0	R. H. E. Jones, Enson House, Llanrhaidr, Oswestry.
4305 Poppy	Bay, 14-2	W. D. Jones, Wernpennant, Llangedwin, Oswestry.
4242 Toffee	Chest., 13-3	E. Lodwick, Rhiwfwar, Llanfyllin.
4301 Polly of Moelfre	Bay, 14-0	H. Morgan, Park, Moelfre, Oswestry.
4303 Polly of Talwrn	Black, 14-0	J. Ellis, Talwrn, Penygarnedd, Llanrhaidr, Oswestry.
4325 Bess of Penybryn	Chest., 15-0	E. Jones, Penybryn, Llanechain.
4330 Fanny of Brynpainod	Chest., 14-2	T. Jones, Brynpainod, Llanfechain.
4294 Pollie of Crychynan	Chest., 14-1	E. Jones, Crychynan Issa, Llanarmon, Ruabon.
4304 Polly of Trewern	Chest., 14-0	E. Evans, Trewern Issa, Llanrhaidr, Oswestry.
4225 Polly of Tyucha	Chest., 13-0	J. Davies, Tyucha, Bwlchyddar, Llangedwin, Oswestry.
4329 Fanny of Brynavon	Dk. Ch. 14-3	W. A. Jehu, Brynavon, Llanfair.
1483 Dane Molly Grey	Grey, 12-2	J. Ellis Jones, Globe House, Llanfyllin.
4318 Verniew Lass	Chest., 14-0	R. Jones, Plas, Dolang, Welshpool.

By 1923 the number of premiums awarded by the Board of Agriculture and Fisheries in England and Wales had increased to ninety comprising eighteen Welsh Cob stallions, three Pembrokeshire Roadster stallions, five riding ponies, five Fells, four Dales, fifteen New Forest and forty Welsh Mountain Ponies and in 1924 the awarding body became the War Office.

By the late twenties the premium scheme was doing sterling work for the furtherance of the Welsh Cob breed, for example, in 1928 there were three premiums each offered in Breconshire, Cardiganshire, Carmarthenshire, Glamorganshire, Montomeryshire, Pembrokeshire and Radnorshire with one each in Denbighsire and Merionethshire. Each premium stallion was listed in the WSB along with the route which he would travel and names of the Local Committee members led by the name of the contact person with whom mare owners would liaise.

1928 Welsh Cob Premium Stallions and their routes

BRECON

Ceitho Welsh Comet (774)
OWNER – Mr S. R. Owen, Tygwyn, Trecastle, Brecon
ROUTE – Brecon: Ystradgynlais and Senny Bridge District

Mathyrafal Brenin (873)
OWNER – Mr D. Rees, Bears Hill Stud Farm, Penuwch, Llanio Road, Cards
ROUTE – Brecon: Brecon, Hay, Talgarth and Crickhowell districts

Ffynonwen Young Defiance (1299)
OWNER – Mr T. Williams, Penbont, Upper Chapel, Brecon
ROUTE – Brecon: Builth and Llanwrtyd Districts

Myrtle Welsh Flyer (1020)
OWNER – Mr T. James, Myrtle Hill, Llechryd
ROUTE – Cardigan (North): Aberystwyth, Llanilar, Lledrod District, Tregaron (Brynawel), Pontrhydfengaid District, Cross Wood, Capel Seion, Bow Street District, Talybont, Llanfarian District, Llanrhystyd

Cefncoch Country Swell (1286)
OWNER – Mrs E. Hughes, Cefncoch, Rhydfelin, Aberystwyth.
ROUTE – Cardigan (Mid): Aberyron, Cilie Aeron, Pennant, Llanon,

Llynhystyd, Cross Inn, Penuwch, Tregaron, Pont Llanio, Llandewi-Brefi, Llanfair, Llwyngroes, Cellan, Lampeter, Llangybi, Llangeitho, Talsarn District, Ystrad, Temple Bar, Cribyn, Capelgroes, Cwrtneydd, Gorsgoch, Mydroilyn, Synod Inn, Llanarth.

Llethi Valiant (1238)
OWNER – Mr J. Richards, Cnwcapedwart, Llanarth, Llandyssul.
ROUTE – Cardigan (South): Newcastle Emlyn, Cardigan, Godeddan, Brynhoffnant, Rhydlewis District, Llandyssul, Talgarreg Synod, Nanternis District, Llwyndafydd District, Llangranog District, Beulah District.

CARMARTHEN

Pistyll Cob (628)
OWNER – Mr D. Davies, Blaenpistill, Cardigan.
ROUTE – Cothy Bridge, Llanfynydd, Llandilo, Llansawel, Llandyssul, Pencader, Pumpsaint, Velingwm.

Matchless Comet of Cefncoch (1138)
OWNER – Mrs E. Hughes, Cefncoch Stud, Rhydfelin.
ROUTE – Carmarthen, St Clears, Mydrin, Treloch, Talog, Cilrhedyn, Whitland, Nantgaredig, Kidwelly.

Gwenog Welsh Flyer (1353)
OWNER – Mr D. Jones, Brookland House, Llanwenog.
ROUTE – Llangadock, Llandovery, New Inn (Gwynfe), Gwynfe Village, Brynamman, Ammanford, Llanedy, Pontardulais, Dyffryn, Ceidrychy, Llanddeusant (Cross Inn).

DENBIGH

Llwyn Dazzler (1387)
OWNERS – Messrs John Jones & Son, Dinarth Hall, Colwyn Bay.
ROUTE – Colwyn Bay, Glan Conway, Eglwysbach, Naenan, Llanrwst, Gwtherin, Llangerniew, Llansannan, Llanefydd, Henllan, Denbigh, St Asaph, Bettws, Abergele, Llanelian.

GLAMORGAN

Mathrafal Flying King (787)
OWNERS – Messrs John John & Sons, Farmers' Arms, Haverfordwest.

ROUTE – Porthcawl, Pyle, Bridgend, Llanharan, Llantrissant, Tonyrefail, Blackmill, Maesteg, Bryn, Margam, Kenfig, Caerau, Cymmer, Cwmdyffryn.

Llanedy Trustful Gambler (1300)
OWNER – Mr W. Owen, Penfedfawr, Llanedy, Pontardulais.
ROUTE – Gorseinon, Three Crosses, Parkmill, Reynoldston, Llangennith, Llanrhidian, Killay, Sketty, Fforestfach, Morriston and Neath.

Blaenwaun True Briton (1351)
OWNER – Mr T. Rees, Blaenwaun Stud Farm, Penuwch, Nr Llanio Road.
ROUTE – Pontypridd, Rhondda, Aberdare, Methyr, Nelson, Llandbradach, Caerphilly, Llantrissant Town and Lisvane.

MERIONETH

Blaenwaun Britonian (878)
OWNER – T. Rees, Esq., Blaenwaun Stud Farm, Penuwch, Nr Llanio Road.
ROUTE – Dolgelley, Machynlleth, Pennal, Towyn, Arthog, Bala, Corwen, Colyn, Trawsfynydd, Maentwrog, Harlech, Barmouth.

MONTGOMERY

Cymro-yr Hafod (1290)
OWNER – Major W. M. Dugdale (Lessee), Llwyn, Llanfyllin.
ROUTE – Llanfyllin, Llantsantffraid, Llanwyddyn and Llanrhaidr.

Mathrafal Eiddwen (965)
OWNER – Mr H. M. Jones, Mathrafal, Meifod.
ROUTE – Newtown, Llandinam, Llanidloes, Llanbrynmair and Cemmaes Road.

Teify Comet (886)
OWNER – The Dinam Estates Co., Llandinam.
ROUTE – Meifod, Welshpool, Berriew, Castle Caerinon, Llanfair, Llanerfyl and Guildsfield.

PEMBROKE

Ceitho Welsh Flyer (1080)
OWNER – Mr W. Howells, Hentbantfach, Penuwch, Nr Llanio Road.
ROUTE – Narberth, Tenby, Pembroke and Lawrenny Districts.

Brechfa Briton Comet (Vol. 22)
OWNER – Mr. T. Williams, Brechfa, Clynderwen, Pembroke.
ROUTE – Haverfordwest, Mildford, Marloes, Maenclochog and Clarbeston Road District.

Pembroke Lad (WR6)
OWNER – Mr G. P. George, Great Nash, Llwgwm, Pembroke.
ROUTE – Newport, Fishguard, St Davids and Letterston.

RADNOR

Leinthall Prince Elwyn (968)
OWNER – Mr J. Davies, The Grange, Glasbury-on-Wye.
ROUTE – Glasbury, Boughrood, Llandilograban, Paincastle, Bryngwyn, Newchurch, Gladwestry, Clyro and Llowes.

Llwynog-y-Mynydd (1239)
OWNER – Mr G. Gittins, Machine House, Presteign, Rads.
ROUTE – Knighton, Whitton, Presteigne, New Radnor, Llanfihangel, Nantmelan, Llandegley, Penybont, Dolau, Bleddfa, Llangunllo, Llanbister Road, Velindre, Beguildy and Knucklass.

Honddu Welsh Warrior (833)
OWNER – Mr T. Williams, Penbont, Upper Chapel, Nr Brecon.
ROUTE – Llandrindod Wells, Hundred House, Llanelwedd, Builth Road, Newbridge-on-Wye, Llanyre, Nantmel, Rhayader, Llananno, Llandewi and Cross Gates.

Included amongst these 1928 stallions are some very famous names in Welsh Cob history including the Royal Welsh Prince of Wales Cup winners: Myrtle Welsh Flyer (1933 and 1939), Llethi Valiant (1931) and Mathrafal Eiddwen (1926, 1927, 1929 and 1930). Ceitho Welsh Comet, though not a Cup winner himself, sired the winners Dewi Black Bess (1935) and Teify of Hercws (1936 and 1937), Mathrafal Brenin won the cup in 1924 and 1925 and, whilst travelling Breconshire in 1928, served Doll to produce in 1929 Cymraes who, when covered by the Rees's other stallion Gwalia Victor in 1935, produced Brenin Gwalia the 1947 Royal Welsh male champion.

The premiums were discontinued in 1930, to the great disappointment of Welsh Cob stallion owners. Captain Howson, Secretary of the

Royal Welsh Agricultural Society and WPCS, writing in the 1932 *Royal Welsh Agricultural Society Journal* states

> The Welsh Cob has been badly hit by the economy campaign which has cut off the premiums – at an expenditure amounting merely to a bagatelle – which did so much to ensure a sufficiency of useful sires. The Welsh Cob is far too valuable a breed to be allowed to join the many other sacrifices on the altar of official lack of vision. In spite of the growth of other means of locomotion, there remain many uses for strong, spanking, lion-hearted Cobs, both in and out of Wales, and it is sincerely to be hoped that those who own good breeding stock of the true and tested lines of blood will, with the patriotism they have always shown, hold on to it until the dawn of those better times which optimists believe will come again. And optimists are not invariably wrong!

These sentiments were reiterated on page 121 of the same *Journal* by Mr Meyrick Jones (Mathrafal) in his Judge's report of the Welsh Pony and Cob classes. Mr Jones had attended every Royal Welsh Show since its inception in 1904 (with one exception) and consequently was in a position to reflect on the ebbs and flows of the previous thirty years. He expresses sadness at the decision of the War Office and Treasury in abolishing the premium grants.

> The withdrawal of the premiums affords a concrete instance of the interests of Welsh farmers being sacrificed in order to help to reduce Army Estimates; and this in spite of the fact that on the outbreak of War in 1914 practically every Welsh mare – whether in foal or not – was speedily taken over for military purposes.

There were small signs of a revival from the 1931 depression by 1934, Captain Howson writing in the 1934 *Royal Welsh Journal*:

> As the fruits of somewhat long drawn-out negotiations between representatives of the Welsh Pony and Cob Society and officials of the Remount Department at the War Office – to whose patience, courtesy and sympathy in our afflictions a tribute must be paid – premiums will be available in the coming spring for Welsh Cob

stallions to travel Breconshire and Radnorshire, Cardiganshire, Glamorgan and Montgomeryshire. The premiums will be fewer in number and less in monetary value than was the case before the panic born of the economic crisis led to their suspension in 1932. But their reinstatement is the great thing and is, we hope, the thin end of the wedge which will result in their full restoration on the old-time scale in the not too far distant future.

It is, we believe, the case that on the outbreak of the World War in 1914, Wales was practically denuded of her Cobs of working age which (even inclusive of a quantity of breeding mares) were commandeered for army purposes in which sphere they carried out the duties set them faithfully and well. This fact, coupled with the future one that the military authorities still have a sympathetic leaning towards him, fortifies the claim of the Welsh Cob to be, per se, an army horse and suitable for army horse production.

It is understood that the whole of the money available from public funds for the encouragement of native breeds in England, Wales and Scotland during 1935 totals only £500 and that that sum is part of the £5,000 voted by the Treasury up to the War office for subsidising stallions for producing a suitable supply of horses for military use. The remainder of the grant (£4,500) plus £5,000 from the Racecourse Betting Control Board is to be devoted to the provision of premiums for blood sires i.e. £9,500 for subsidising thoroughbreds compared with a paltry £500 for stallions of all the native breeds combined!.

The renewal of the premium grants, though smaller than before, gave rise to a small degree of optimism; four premiums each of £25 were offered to Cob stallions during 1935, concentrating on the counties with the highest numbers of breeding mares. Eighteen stallions were presented before judges Mr Tom Jones Evans and Mr E. G. E. Griffith. Gwalia Victor travelled around Radnorshire and Breconshire and covered ninety-eight mares but this resulted in a disappointing number of foals: Myrtle Welsh Flyer served fifty-one mares in Cardiganshire (twenty-eight foals), Llanedy Trustful Gambler served forty-six mares in Glamorgan (eighteen foals) and Gwenog Briton Lad served twenty-seven mares in Montgomeryshire (fifteen foals).

The grant for 1936 was increased to £175 which was divided into five premiums of £35 each, the fifth being awarded to Pembrokeshire. The judges, again Mr Tom Jones Evans and Mr Eddie Griffith, were joined by Brigadier R. Carrington, the Assistant Director of Remounts, on their visits to the five counties to inspect the stallions. Of the £35, £20 was awarded when the stallion was selected and the remaining £15 when the stallion service book was delivered to the WPCS at the end of the season. The maximum service fee which could be charged by the premium stallion owners was £1.10.0.

The premium scheme was maintained during the war years with three or four travelling premiums awarded each year. Six premiums were awarded in 1946, with Cardiganshire warranting two (one each for North and South), an additional premium for Anglesey but no premium for Glamorganshire from 1937 to 1948.

Rather than have the judges travelling around the counties, on 6 April 1956 twelve stallions congregated at Lampeter to compete for eight premiums of £80 and were judged as a show class. This was won by Llwynog-y-Garth who was awarded a premium for Monmouthshire.

Llwynog-y-Garth, winner at the first Lampeter Show 1956. Photo by Wynne Davies.

BRENIN GWALIA (1934-1965)

Painting by Robert Thwaites of many-times premium stallion Brenin Gwalia with owner David Rees (1892–1969) riding, Brynarth Titch leading the stallion. Note: stallion's food attached to his girth. David Rees's father Thomas Rees (right) with hat and pipe and son (left) John Roderick Rees. Courtesy of Roy Tidman.

There was a large attendance of interested spectators who were charged one shilling admission. In order to attract more spectators, additional classes were offered for section A, B and C stallions with prize money supplied by the Horse and Pony Breeding and Benefit Committee in addition to the five travelling premiums of £120 each for Welsh Cob stallions using funds provided by the Racecourse Betting Levy Board. These arrangements continued until 1962 when the Show was taken over by a Lampeter Local Committee providing facilities for the allocation of four Welsh Cob premiums of £40 each awarded to stallions standing at home. By 1969 the entries at Lampeter had increased to 138 in fourteen classes, the Welsh Cob premiums being one each of £100 for a stallion standing at Stud in North Wales (three entries) and South Wales (five entries) and two for Mid-Wales (fourteen entries).

Comparative figures for the 1995 Lampeter Show were a total of 604 entries in twenty-nine classes, eight Cob stallions competed for two premiums of £300 each for North Wales won by Trevallion Ace Comet, twenty-three stallions for six premiums of £300 each for South Wales won by Ebbw Viscount who was also champion and eighteen stallions for six premiums of £300 for Mid-Wales won by Gellifach ap Dafydd who was later champion at the 1995 Royal Welsh Show. These fourteen stallions covered 310 mares in 1995, the largest number being the fifty-one covered by Tyreos Valentino who stood third in the South Wales class. In addition eight premiums of £300 were awarded to stallions standing at Stud in England and Scotland, these being judged at Shows held in the respective areas.

When the stallions were 'travelled' around the various counties, their leaders would be astride mares walking an average of twenty-five miles per day. Pictured (opposite) is the stallion Brenin Gwalia (travelling premiums every year from 1942 to 1953) with owner David Rees riding Brynarth Titch, who carried him unstintingly for fifteen consecutive years.

CHAPTER FOUR

Welsh Cob auction sales

FOLLOWING ON FROM the successes of the Fayre Oaks Sale for Welsh Mountain ponies and Welsh ponies, section B, it was the brainchild of the late Miss Pauline Taylor of the Llanarth Stud to hold a similar sale for Welsh Cobs and Welsh ponies of Cob-type, section C.

The first Fayre Oaks Sale was held on 9 October 1954 when seventy-six ponies were catalogued and this number had increased to 411 by the 1964 Sale. The first Llanarth Sale was held at the Llanarth Stud, Blaenwern Farm, Llanarth Cardiganshire on 17 October 1964, Miss Taylor selecting St Luke's ('Little Summer') Day in the hope of fine weather since it was an 'open air' sale with animals from outside vendors having to stay in their own conveyances on a boggy field! No great numbers were expected since, although Welsh pony and Cob annual registration numbers had increased from around 500 in 1954 to 1,820 in 1964, the comparative percentages of Cobs had decreased (1954: 86 per cent A; 4 per cent B; 1 per cent C; 9 per cent D) to 4 per cent (with 75 per cent A) in 1964. However sixty-two lots were offered at the first Sale where the auctioneers were jointly Russell, Baldwin and Bright and J. J. Morris of Cardigan, the former being sole auctioneers after 1968.

Forty of the sixty-two lots were sold, twenty section Ds averaging 122 guineas and seven section Cs averaging 105 guineas, which were very encouraging prices in view of the nation-wide financial stringency prevailing at that time. The top figure of the sale was 300 guineas, paid by Yorkshire pioneer Welsh Cob breeder Mrs Betty Sowerby of the Arth Stud for Llanarth Stud's yearling palomino Cob filly Llanarth Sissel, daughter of the famous Llanarth Flying Saucer, whose other progeny include the multi-champion, Llanarth Flying Comet, Llanarth Meteor (sire of Friskney Frolic top of the 1992 sale) and Australian champion Llanarth Jack Flash. Twenty-three of the sixty-two lots were from Llanarth Stud, the star 'outside' lot being that year's Royal Welsh winning yearling colt Teify King which sold for 210 guineas.

There was nothing outstanding at the 1965 sale. Two mares which did not reach their very modest reserves at the 1966 sale were Llanarth Stud's Llanarth Lady Valiant and Derwen Stud's Derwen Groten Ddu. With hindsight, these were very wise decisions on the part of the vendors since Lady Valiant in 1976 produced the top sire Llanarth True Briton and Groten Ddu in 1981 produced the 1986, 1990 and 1992 Royal Welsh champion Derwen Groten Goch. The day before the 1967 sale, an increase in the bank lending rate was announced which did not encourage breeders; however there was a steady trade for the best, Llanarth Sissel who proved a little small for the Arth Stud being re-sold for 330 guineas and the good sixteen-year-old mare Hwylog Eiddwen being sold to start the Dwyfor Stud (winners of the 1997 Champagne Moment) at 280 guineas. Hwylog Eiddwen came from a very old strain, her g-g-dam Hwylog Polly being foaled in 1896; her half-sister Hwylog Briallen is g-dam of the 1990 Royal Welsh champion, Thorneyside the Boss, the 1992 Royal Welsh champion, Thorneyside Flyer, and also Thorneyside More Magic, top of the 1989 sale at 6,000 guineas. Twenty-eight Cobs from a total catalogue entry at the 1968 sale sold for an average of £133, Miss Anne Wheatcroft paying 500 guineas for the six-year-old mare Tyhen Dainty, the daughter of the 1962 and 1973 Royal Welsh champion Tyhen Mattie.

Greatest interest at the 1969 sale centred around the two dun sisters, Chancerie Mist and Chancerie Iris, whose other sister, Chancerie Polly, was dam of the many-times champion, Hewid Cardi. These mares sold for 300 and 310 guineas, with Dyfi Pride also selling for 310 guineas to an American, Samuel King of New York, this heralding the start of a very lucrative current trade for Cobs to the United States, where previously only section As had been sold in any appreciable numbers. Of the total catalogue entry of 115, sixty were Cobs, thirty-eight of them selling for 4,985 guineas; an average of £131. Numbers at the 1970 sale were up to 132 (still very small compared with the 910 offered at the 1970 Fayre Oaks Sale). Top of the sale at 350 guineas was the yearling filly, Poppit Myfanwy, who returned to top the 1982 Llanarth Sale at 1,000 guineas. Llanarth Valmai created some excitement when she sold for 330 guineas, the best price so far for any foal. The four-year-old Broughton Ivy fetched only 225 guineas to go to start the Ffoslas Stud; her daughter, Ffoslas Black Lady, was champion of the 1979 Royal Welsh Show and g-g-daughter Ffoslas Lady Model (filly foal) sold for 4,200 guineas at the 1994 Royal Welsh Sale, the second-highest figure ever for a filly foal. It was at the 1971 sale that figures started their meteoric rise, when 104 Cobs sold for an average of £187. Cefncoch Gwenogwen set a new record of 500 guineas for a filly foal; Tyhen Stud came out tops again with Tyhen Ffafret (two-year-old) and Tyhen Dandy both selling for 400 guineas. Three of the top lots were paid for with a stolen cheque and left the sale in a stolen horsebox but fortunately were traced and four men were charged at Aberaeron Magistrates Court the following January and sent to prison. The increase in prices was even more dramatic at the 1972 sale with the average increasing from £187 in 1971 to £290 in 1972 and a sale total of £39,505; a ten-fold increase on the first sale's total of £3,744.

There were fourteen good mares on offer who averaged 505 guineas, Tyhen Stud again being top, selling the four-year-old Tyhen Princess for 1,400 guineas. Llanarth Stud themselves also hit the jackpot; the first foal to fetch 1,000 guineas was their Llanarth Mari, full-sister to the well-known Llanarth Meredith ap Braint.

The increase in average prices continued at the 1973 sale. Despite the atrocious weather (the first wet day for ten years), 127 Cobs (from a total catalogue entry of 298) averaged £337, with nineteen mares finding the best trade and averaging £577. The seven-year-old black mare Geler Eirlys, daughter of the 1964 Royal Welsh champion, Geler Daisy, topped the sale at 1,100 guineas. Parc Brigadier, a colt foal, son of four-times Royal Welsh champion Parc Rachel, sold for 400 guineas; the next time he re-appeared at the Llanarth Sale (1980) he set up a record of 3,000 guineas which held until 1987.

There was nothing very exciting at the 1974 sale, consequently the average fell to £219 and the average for the 1975 sale was about the same (£231) despite a good export trade, with seventeen sold to Germany and four to Holland. Derwen Stud paid 850 guineas for the ten-year-old black mare, Rhandir Margarita, full-sister to Derwen Rosina with which they had won the Royal Welsh championships in 1966, 1967 and 1968. Promising colt foals found a better trade, Roy Higgins receiving 700 guineas for Tireinon Shooting Star (which had won at the Royal Welsh) and Derwen Romeo sold for 620 guineas; Derwen Stud bought him back in 1987 to go to Sweden.

The Llanarth site was bursting at the seams, with 285 lots catalogued and in 1975 Russell, Baldwin and Bright arranged the first 'Royal Welsh Sale' two weeks before the Llanarth Sale, with 234 sections A and B offered on the first day ('overflow' for the Fayre Oaks Sale) and 161 sections C and D on the second day and they found plenty of interest for a 'first time experiment'. One colt sold there was Medley Jupitor (120 guineas); he became a consistent winner including second to Ebbw Victor out of thirty-one at the 1983 Royal Welsh Show.

By 1976 the Llanarth Farms and Stud had become the property of the University College of Wales, Aberystwyth, who allowed the sale to continue there for another six years, after which they sold the farm and dispersed the stud. The 344 entries at the 1976 Llanarth Sale were mainly from within the Principality, with 'outside' entries being encouraged to enter for the Royal Welsh Sale. Overseas visitors boosted the 1976

John Williams and Medley Jupitor being presented to Her Majesty The Queen at the 1983 R W Show (HRH The Duke of Edinburgh with the author on left of photo).

73

Llanarth Sale when Canadian P. A. Carter paid 1,600 guineas for the yearling colt, Derwen Arwr, a new male record. Derwen Stud reached even greater heights at the 1977 sale by securing the two top prices, 1,500 guineas for the yearling colt Derwen Trysor and 1,400 guineas for the filly foal Derwen's Last Request. From 283 catalogued, 157 Cobs sold for an average of £316 with a Sale total of £58,327. Top adult female was the Royal Agricultural Society of England winner, Arthen Bernadette, which Trevallion Stud sold for 1,100 guineas to Cyttir Stud, her resulting 1978 colt foal Cyttir Telynor fetching 380 guineas at the Royal Welsh Sale to Fronarth Stud, who won the 1987 Royal Welsh championship with him, and he became one of the current leading sires. 1978 was a memorable year as far as Welsh Pony and Cob Sales were concerned, section As had sold to 21,000 guineas at the Coed Coch Dispersal Sale (total: £184,453) and eighty-five section As and Bs sold on the Western Reduction Sale for £52,116. Cobs at the 1978 Llanarth Sale rose from £316 average in 1977 to £388 (23 per cent) while at the Royal Welsh Sale the increase was a staggering 79 per cent (£206 to £369). The 2,000-guineas mark was reached for the first time when Dr June Alexander of the Okeden Stud in Yorkshire paid 2,300 guineas for the five-year-old mare Rhystyd Mattie at Llanarth Sale. The Rhystyd Stud of the Rowlands Harris family is steeped in Welsh Cob history, standing the Cob stallion Cardigan Rainbow at stud in 1887. Mattie was sired by the 1966 and 1969 Royal Welsh champion, Tyhen Comet, who at that time was at the Trevallion Stud. The stud's own yearling colt, Trevallion Flash Jack, sold for 1,800 guineas to top the males. Derwen Stud again topped the foals with Derwen Dyma Hi selling for 1,300 guineas.

The 1979 sales coincided with the setting-up of the Welsh part-bred breeding centre at the Warwickshire College of Agriculture and the College Principal, Mr Graham Suggett, attended the Llanarth Sale personally to select the future stud stallion, buying the yearling colt Llanarth Black Jack for 2,000 guineas, the first male to reach that figure at these sales. Black Jack sired some useful animals at 'Warcolag' with foals selling well at the Royal Welsh Sales from about 1983 onwards. The Llanarth site had reached its capacity with 300 lots offered and a turnover of £82,010 which was good, considering that fifty-eight of the lots were colt foals.

The 1979 Royal Welsh Sale had now overtaken the Llanarth Sale in terms of numbers (325) with some 'Wales' vendors dividing their entries

between the two sales to save on transport, handlers and so on. Prices at the Royal Welsh Sale were also catching up, helped by ten sold to Germany and two to Holland. While 326 proved to be the absolute maximum that the 1980 Llanarth Sale could entertain (decreased to 171 in 1982), the numbers at the Royal Welsh increased from 143 to 1977 to 400 in 1980. Parc Brigadier, who had sold for 400 guineas as a foal at Llanarth, re-appeared and fetched 3,000 guineas to FEI driver David Cripps, a record which was to hold for the next eight years. The five-year-old mare Penllwynuchel Wendy sold for 1,900 guineas, the second-highest female figure to date. Interest in geldings as all-round riding animals was beginning and Trevallion Stud had 1,100 guineas for recently backed Trevallion Bright Boy at three years old. With the introduction of 'upset' price at Llanarth, 131 of them were not sold but 70 per cent sold at the Royal Welsh Sale, where there were no 'upset' prices. In the same way that the Coed Coch Dispersal Sale of 1978 can be described as the 'sale of the century' as far as Welsh ponies are

Derwen Dyma Hi, top of the foals (1,300 guineas) at the 1978 Llanarth Sale. Photo, when owned by Mrs Rose Hardwick, winning at the Three Counties Show.

concerned, the first Derwen Stud Reduction Sale held on 26 September 1981 can be regarded as a very special event for Welsh Cobs. Thirty-two Cobs were offered by auction and when one considers that twenty of them were foals (eight fillies and twelve colts) the average figure of £801 was quite remarkable, especially when compared with the Cob averages of £382 at Llanarth and £336 at the Royal Welsh. It took up to 1990 for the average of £801 to be overtaken at a Royal Welsh Sale but, to keep up with inflation, the £801 in 1981 would have been about £1,400 in 1990.

It was a gelding, Derwen King Last, who stole the show at the 1981 Derwen Sale, selling for 1,900 guineas. The black five-year-old mare Derwen Perl topped the mares at 1,500 guineas, a very beautiful daughter of the magnificent Derwen Princess, the 1982, 1983 and 1984 Royal Welsh champion. Perl came back to the 1989 Royal Welsh Sale selling to Peter Gray of the Thorneyside Stud for 4,400 guineas, re-appearing again at the 1993 sale, after producing two foals at Thorneyside, selling for 4,000 guineas despite being seventeen years old, her last United Kingdom appearance since she was sold to the United States largest importer, Suzanne Glenn of the Glenhaven Stud, California. Sue Howe of the Marl Stud paid a record 1,400 guineas for the colt foal, Rhuban Glas; he took over stud duties from their Olympia ridden champion, Wiston Llwynog, and is still a sire much in demand especially for artificial insemination to overseas countries.

There were 253 lots entered for the 1981 Llanarth Sale which returned the good average of £382 but, owing to the application of 'upset' figures, eighty-seven lots were unsold. Miss Pauline Taylor, who had always given all visitors to the sale such a warm welcome, had died but the Llanarth flag was kept flying when Llanarth Dolly topped the foals at 800 guineas and Llanarth Valiants Image was the top stallion at 2,000 guineas.

The average at the 1981 Royal Welsh Sale was less (£311) but the percentage sold (77 per cent) was much higher and this was the first time for the Royal Welsh Sale total (£74,035) to exceed that of the Llanarth Sale (£55,893), although the top prices at Llanarth were higher than those at the Royal Welsh, thirty mares sold for over 500 guineas at the Royal Welsh compared with fifteen at Llanarth. Tom Evans of Cathedine who had made a habit of selling the top foal at the Royal Welsh Sale sold Cathedine Pure Maid for his highest price to date, 1,300 guineas and he was to buy her back for 3,400 guineas when she came back to the 1988 Royal Welsh Sale.

The 1982 Derwen Sale was a collective sale with 113 Cobs offered and sixty-seven sold with a top figure of 1,000 guineas for the filly foal, Derwen Queen of Hearts. The weather for the 1982 Llanarth Sale was the worst ever, which unfortunately was reflected in the prices, with only eighty-one out of the total of 154 (52 per cent) finding new owners. Poppit Myfanwy who had topped the 1970 Llanarth Sales as a yearling in 1970 again came out on top at 1,000 guineas and Llanarth Stud topped the foals with Llanarth Mefys at 800 guineas. The average price was down to £272, which was a sad ending to the last Llanarth Collective Sale.

Of the 336 lots offered (409 catalogued) at the 1982 Royal Welsh Sale 261 sold for a total of £82,251, that is an average of £300 with 198 Cobs sold (78 per cent) for an average of £317. Top of the sale at 1,400 guineas was the ten-year-old stallion, Kilgour Welsh Monarch, bought by Rod Rees; Monarch died suddenly in October 1995 after escaping and getting to the food store; however for Rod he sired the spectacular 1993

Kilgour Welsh Monarch on parade in front of TV cameras at the International Show, Ermelo, Holland in 1984. Photo by Tegwyn Price.

Royal Welsh champion, Horeb Euros, always a firm favourite with show-goers. Two full-sisters, Elli Queen and Elli Princess, were bought by Hans Strelin for 1,200 guineas each and Mr Strelin derived great pleasure from driving them as a pair in Holland right up to his death at the age of ninety in October 1997.

The 24th of September 1983 was a very sad day in the history of the Welsh Cob. Blaenwern Farm and the Llanarth Welsh Cob Stud, which had been the gift of the late Misses Enid Lewis and Pauline Taylor on the condition that it would never be sold, was on offer – the Cobs, cattle, sheep and implements (the farm already having been sold). The total of twenty-five mares, fillies, foals and geldings sold for a total of £15,084 (an average of £603) with two stallions, seven mares and three yearling fillies being retained by the University at their Frongoch Farm, Aberystwyth. Llanarth Sue Ellen, a four-year-old chestnut daughter of Llanarth True Briton and Llanarth Sian topped the sale at 1,700 guineas and she stayed in Wales. Two filly foals also sold to Welsh breeders, Llanarth Rhadlon (950 guineas to Mr James of Whitland) and Llanarth Ffion at 925 guineas to Paith Stud where she remained until sold for 4,500 guineas at the 1993 Royal Welsh Sale.

Llanarth Sue Ellen at the Llanarth Dispersal Sale: 24 Sept 1983. Photo by Pfeiffer Photographic.

For 1983 the Derwen and Royal Welsh Sales were combined into one catalogue, Derwen Sale taking place at the usual Llanarth Sale date. The weather at the Derwen Sale was atrocious; only seventy-seven of the 138 animals were sold and the weather reduced the average price to £251; this fact, coupled with the enormous work involved at Derwen Stud to stage a collective sale, heralded the last of the Derwen and Llanarth outdoor sales. Top of the Derwen Sale at 1,000 guineas was Tewgoed Magic Lady, also bought by Mr Strelin. Tewgoed Magic Lady's two sisters Tewgoed Mari and Tewgoed Janet are well-known names in Wales. Now owned by Nebo Stud, Mari is dam of the 1994 Royal Welsh Champion, Nebo Hywel, and Janet is dam of Nebo Thomas, who was youngstock champion at the same show.

Llanarth Ffion reappearing at the 1993 sale where she topped the sale at 4,500 guineas. Photo by Wynne Davies.

Of the 420 animals catalogued for the 1983 Royal Welsh Sale, 377 appeared and 276 (72 per cent) were sold for a sale average of £313. Performance animals were most in demand, the ridden three-year-old filly, Ross Black Bess, selling for the top price of 1,300 guineas and the driven three-year-old gelding, Tewgoed Flyer, fetching 1,050 guineas.

The final 1983 Cob sale was the Gwenfo Stud Dispersal Sale, Londoner Mr Mitchell buying the top-priced eleven-year-old mare Gwenfo Flicka for 640 guineas, having already sold her daughter, Gwenfo Beauty, to top the 1981 Royal Welsh Sale at 1,450 guineas. Mr Mitchell also bought the stallion, Gwenfo Apollo, for 460 guineas and won many Royal Welsh harness classes with him. The 1968 Royal Welsh champion Rhystyd Prince sold for 360 guineas at twenty-three years old and Geraint Brynawelon (full-brother to Thorneyside Stud top sire Brenin Brynawelon) sold for 250 guineas at seventeen years old.

With the continuous downpours in October 1984 it was a great relief that the 1984 Royal Welsh Sale was held indoors and with 437 entries, it was extended to two days. There were several exciting animals on offer, interested spectators/purchasers thronged the ring eight or ten deep, the average figure was up 28 per cent to £400 and unusually, males dominated the top positions. Tireinon Triple Crown topped the sale at 2,200 guineas as a three-year-old; he later returned to the Royal Welsh

Gwenfo Apollo sold for 460 guineas at the 1983 Gwenfo Dispersal Sale. Photo by Arthur Thompson.

Showground to win the harness class in 1989. Triple Crown is a brother to Tireinin Shooting Star top foal at the 1975 Llanarth Sale and it was a Shooting Star son who fetched the second-highest price of 1,900 guineas; this was the yearling Cascob Secret Agent, sold by Cascob Stud, where Shooting Star was senior sire. Top female also at 1,900 guineas was the three-year-old filly Graigifan Miss Taylor, daughter of Derwen Dyma Hi, the top foal at the 1978 sale and which Derwen Stud later bought back at the 1990 sale. Llanarth Sue Ellen, top of the Llanarth Dispersal Sale the previous year came back on the market due to the death of her purchaser and fetched 1,150 guineas, only to re-appear at the 1990 sale to sell for 2,000 guineas. Animals who were later to make a name for themselves at their new homes were: Penllwynuchel Hedydd to Moelgwyn Stud, Corscaron Moonlight to Tardebigge Stud, Berthedith Sue Ellen (daughter of Llanarth Sue Ellen) to Broughton Stud, Pantlleinau Myfanwy to Bronfoel Stud from where her daughter, Bronfoel Boneddiges Mai, sold for 5,000 guineas at the 1994 sale.

With the 1984 sale having given much encouragement to breeders, there were 600 animals entered for the 1985 Royal Welsh Sale and the average of £401 received for the 364 sold was very satisfactory in view of the large number of colt foals present. Top price at the sale was 2,000 guineas paid by German breeder Mr Reipen for the three-year-old colt, Menai Welsh Sparkler, who went to join his brother, Menai Modern Comet. There was a good selection of top-class mares on offer, sixty-seven of them selling for over 500 guineas (compared with twenty-five in 1982) with Ystrad-Dewi Margarita topping the sale at 1,700 guineas to Bronfoel Stud. Margarita is dam of the many-times champions Ystrad-Dewi Duchess and Brenhines (Rainhill Stud, Reading). Rainhill Stud bought the top colt foal Cathedine Tywysog for 600 guineas while the top filly Tynybryn Gay Go Lady, daughter of Nebo Daniel, at 1,300 guineas was more than twice the figure received for any other foal.

A first for any Sale were the twin filly foals, Paith Magical Blossom and Paith Magical Bloom, their grand-sires being two Royal Welsh champions, Llanarth Braint and Nebo Black Magic. Another record set in 1985 for any Llanarth or Royal Welsh Sale, which was to remain unbroken for three years, was 1,350 guineas received for the gelding Ffald Baron, sired by Kilgour Welsh Monarch (top of the 1982 sale) out of Ceulan Elsa, which I sold to the Ffald Stud as a foal.

Despite the absence of 'high-flyer' four-figure foals from the 1986 Royal Welsh Sale, the average figures compared favourably with previous years, boosted by fifteen male and forty-nine female Cobs selling for over 500 guineas. The top price of 2,200 guineas was paid for the nine-year-old Llanfair May Lady, sired by Parc Dafydd out of a Parc Welsh Flyer daughter; she went to found Claire Willis-Burton's Pentrefelin Stud. Paith Stud, who were second-top with Paith Tywysoges-y-Traeth at 1,500 guineas in 1985 were again second-highest with Paith Spring Blossom at 1,400 guineas.

Both male and female records were broken at the 1987 and 1988 Royal Welsh Sales, the female record of 2,300 guineas (Rhystyd Mattie in 1978) being almost doubled when Tally Wendy sold for 4,000 guineas, having been bought from her breeder for 720 guineas on the 1981 sale. She was certainly a bargain when Elfed Isaac bought her for 2,250 guineas at her next sale appearance in 1991. The top male again was sold to Mr Reipen; this was the three-year-old colt, Penycrug Telynor, who sold for 1,550 guineas and became a top sire in Germany. Tynybryn Bobby Dazzler, full-brother to the 1985 top filly, Tynybryn Gay Go Lady, was far-and-away top colt foal at 1,400 guineas to start a good run of Tynybryn sale-topping foals: Tynybryn What's Wanted (top colt in 1989),

Tynybryn Welsh Maid (second highest filly in 1991) and Tynybryn Lady Express (third highest filly in 1993).

Top of the filly foals, selling for more than twice any other (1,450 guineas), was Synod Rosary, bought by Fronarth Stud, for whom she has produced some exceptional foals such as Fronarth Rosaleen, who sold for 2,800 guineas at the 1994 Royal Welsh Sale. Rosary is sired by Brynymor Welsh Magic (sire also of the Royal Welsh champions Thorneyside The Boss and Thorneyside Flyer) out of Synod Rosemary, possibly the best Cob mare at Synod and winner at the Royal Welsh Royal Agricultural Society of England, Lampeter Rosemary, who died in 1997, leaves a dynasty of champions all over the world including Rembrandt champion in Denmark, Rosie O'Grady champion in the United States, the two famous brothers, Reflection and Rambo (sold for 10,000 guineas at the 1997 sale), and Robert Black, sire of Synod Ruby Black top Cob foal, also at the 1997 sale.

Derwen Ruth (wearing number 905) winning the 1988 RW Show in the presence of HRH The Prince of Wales, seen here discussing the class with the judge Mrs Alison Mountain. Photo by Petra Donath, Switzerland.

By any standards the 1987 sale was a fantastic success; with South-East England suffering the worst gale damage in living memory that week-end and severe flooding having washed away many bridges, seventy-four of the 476 lots failed to arrive at Builth Wells. Of those present 310 (77 per cent) sold for a total of £156,463, so for the first time ever for a Royal Welsh Sale, the average was over £500 (£504) and on its way to reach the peak of £912 in 1990.

If records were broken in 1987, they were blown 'sky high' at the 1988 Royal Welsh Sale, which produced a male record yet to be equalled. It is seldom that a reigning champion stallion is offered for sale by auction, but here to sell was the seven-year-old bay stallion Mabnesscliffe Survivor, many times champion and featured highly in the WPCS sire ratings. There was great excitement when he was knocked down at 10,400 guineas to Brian Hughes, owner of his sire Craignant Flyer, with Peter Gray of Thorneyside (who bought five mares) as under-bidder. Survivor's dam is Hewid Wendy, daughter of Gerrig Stud's Hewid Cardi and her dam is Hewid Melda, dam of many-times champion, Gerrig Glory. Melda's dam is Hewid Delia, sold for 1,600 guineas at the 1981 Llanarth Sale and she is full-sister to Hewid Nesta, g-dam of the 1994 Royal Welsh champion, Nebo Hywel. Survivor certainly lived up to his reputation in his new home, both as a sire and in the show ring being in

Mabnesscliffe Survivor, sold for a record of 10,400 guineas on the 1988 Sale. Photo by Wynne Davies.

the top six stallions (from sixty or more) at three Royal Welsh Shows, as well as champion at the 1994 Glanusk Show.

We have already met Cathedine Pure Maid, sold by her breeder at the 1981 sale but bought back for 3,400 guineas to top the females on the 1988 sale, a wise re-purchase since her breeder, Tom Evans sold her 1992 filly foal, Cathedine May Princess, for 3,000 guineas.

The top-priced colt and filly foals both came from the Aberystwyth area, William and Dafydd Harris selling their Pennal Calon Lan to Abergavenny Stud for 1,000 guineas and Tom and Dafydd Morris selling Neuaddparc Flyer's Model, daughter of Cippyn Red Flyer for 1,100 guineas. Another smart colt foal was Craignant Express; snapped up by Fronarth Stud for 750 guineas, he won enormous classes at the Lampeter Breed Show every year from 1989 to 1991, being twice youngstock champion. There was also good trade for ridden part-breds and geldings, Parvadean Stud paying 1,700 guineas for a three-year-old filly, Cascob

Pennal Calon Lan, top colt foal at 1,000 guineas at the 1988 sale with purchaser Mr John Batt.

Second Chance, sired by Nebo Dafydd out of a Thoroughbred eventing mare and Miss Arabella Ashley (of Laura Ashley) paying 2,400 guineas for the gelding, Talhaearn Flyer, son of Derwen Replica. Altogether 384 animals sold for just over £225,000 – an average of £586 – almost double that attained five years previously.

It was the turn of the female record to be exceeded at the 1989 Royal Welsh Sale. The top price at the sale was 6,000 guineas for the four-year-old home-bred stallion, Thorneyside More Magic, sired by Brynymor Welsh Magic, whose stock had topped so many previous sales. There were many very good brood mares on offer, which were largely responsible for boosting the average by 33 per cent from £586 to £791, the numbers of mares selling for £1,000 or more increasing from one in 1980 to three in 1982, five in 1985, seven in 1986, fourteen in 1987, twenty-six in 1988 and sixty-seven in 1989! The seven-year-old Fronarth Black Diamond topped the mares at 4,500 guineas, her new owner Helen Williams of the Seiont Stud winning a second prize out of fifty-three entries at the Royal Welsh Show the following year, her colt foal Seiont Gwern by Ceredigion Tywysog winning his class.

It has already been quoted in respect of the 1981 Derwen Sale that Derwen Perl, sold that day for 1,500 guineas, was sold to Peter Gray, vendor of the top stallion, for 4,400 guineas. Mr Swain sold his three-year-old filly Botvyle April Moon for 4,000 guineas to Mrs Colls of Darwen, Lancashire; sadly Mrs Colls died in 1990 but Les Colls kept the mare on and qualified her for the Mountain and Moorland Ridden Championships at Olympia in 1994 ending up fifth from thirty against all other British native breeds. Tynybryn What's Wanted was top colt foal at 1,775 guineas and Morlyn Charlie Girl top of the filly foals at 1,600 guineas. With so much encouragement from the 1989 sale, 1990 Royal Welsh Sale entries increased to 918, necessitating an expansion into

Tynbryn What's Wanted, top colt foal at 1,775 guineas, 1988 sale.

three days. Large numbers usually result in decreased demand but fortunately this was not the case for the Welsh Cob, the average going up another 15 per cent to £912 and the sale total increasing by a staggering 48 per cent to £531,027.

Demand was again strongest for the best breeding mares, 95 of them selling for 1,000 guineas or more with a top price of 6,200 guineas for the eight-year-old chestnut Calerux Anniversary sold by John Evans of Glantraeth Stud whose parents had the Tan Lan Stud in the forties. She was sold to Jesse Penfold of the Gristhills Stud, her yearling son Gristhills Malibu Boy being the leading winner in 1994 and is now becoming a top sire. Mr Tony Courtney of Cwrtevan Stud paid 6,000 guineas for the eight-year-old stallion Leyeswick Daniel and won five championships with him in 1991 as well as the Reserve Championship at the International Show in 1992. Mr Courtney's purchases (eleven Cobs) cost him over £28,000, but he was to pay even higher prices the following year! Eighteen filly foals sold for 1,000 guineas or more, which was almost unbelievable when one considers the top price of 400 guineas in 1986. Cathedine Stud produced another sale topper when their Cathedine April Sunshine sold for 3,400 guineas.

Mr Courtney did not let the 1990 female record of 6,200 guineas be upheld for long, at the 1991 Royal Welsh Sale he paid 6,800 guineas for

Leyeswick Daniel, sold for 6,000 guineas, 1990 sale. Photo by Wynne Davies.

Cathedine April Sunshine, sold for 3,400 guineas, more than twice the previous record, 1990 sale. Photo by Wynne Davies.

Pantanamlwg Eleri in foal to the vendor's own Pantanamlwg Red Fox, the Royal Welsh Champion that year. Mabnesscliffe Welsh Model, full-sister to the male record holder Mabnesscliffe Survivor beat the previous foal record of 3,400 guineas by 41 per cent to set up the new record of 4,800 guineas. Exports also held up well, thirty-one sold to Germany, nine to Ireland, three each to France, Austria and Holland and two each to Denmark and Belgium.

The sale total at the 1992 Royal Welsh Sale was down some £50,000 to £460,827 but this was due to 105 fewer animals catalogued, the average over the three days increasing as buyers gained confidence: £654, £734 and £959, giving an overall average almost the same as the previous year at £789. Friskney Frolic, a good-winning harness mare from Northern Ireland topped the sale at 5,500 guineas selling to David Smith of the Broughton Stud whose Broughton Black Lady was champion Cob at the International Show earlier that year. The black

Pantanamlwg Eleri with purchaser Mr Tony Courtney (6,800 guineas) 1991 sale. Photo by Pleasure Prints.

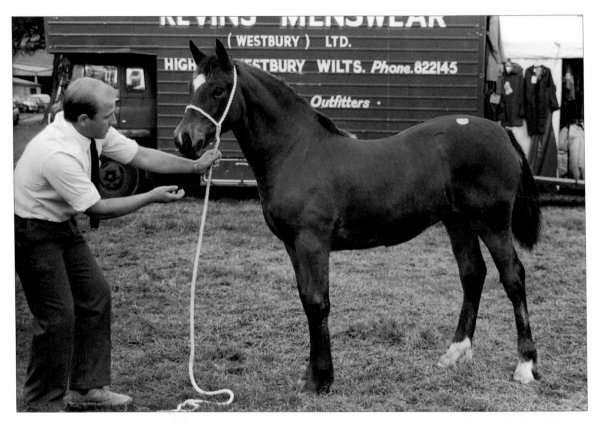

ABOVE *Mabnesscliffe Welsh Model, record priced foal (4,800 guineas) 1991 sale. Photo by Pleasure Prints.*

Friskney Frolic, top-priced mare (5,500 guineas) 1992 sale. Photo by Wynne Davies.

twelve-year-old stallion Ffoslas Sir Gwynfor and the bay yearling colt Thorneyside The Gaffer shared male honours, both selling for 5,000 guineas.

The 1991 Sale total was overtaken at the 1993 Royal Welsh Sale to total £518,876, the second-highest ever, also the second highest average of £853 and the second-highest ever in terms of numbers sold. Two eleven-year-old stallions topped the sale at 5,000 guineas: Leyeswick Daniel, who had been bought for 6,000 guineas in 1990, and Mrs Bridget Wessely's Cathedine Express, whose show ring successes included the supreme championship of the Lampeter Stallion Show, reserve male champion at the Royal Welsh and champion at the Three Counties and Royal Bath and West. It was hoped that he would be a top sire at his new home, Glantraeth Stud but it was not to be as he died suddenly the following spring.

The highest price for females was 4,800 guineas bid for Steve Everitt's black six-year-old mare Navestock Princess but the purchaser gave a fictitious name and address but fortunately failed to take his 'purchases' from the sale precinct; Navestock Princess was later sold privately. Fronarth Tywysoges Wendy who topped the filly foals at 3,000 guineas was a direct descendant of the original foundation mare of the Fronarth Stud, Brynarth Pride foaled in 1948. Close on her heels at 2,900 guineas was Abercippyn Saran, sired by Craignant Flyer, a favourite stallion with David Edwards of Abercippyn out of Pantyfid Actress bred by Abercippyn neighbour Shirley Williams. Owing to the imposition of an 'upset price' that is, a minimum starting bid of £300 on all lots offered, including foals, at the 1994 Royal Welsh Sale the percentage sold was reduced to 64 per cent (563 animals from 885 offered and the sale total reduced from £518,876 to £443,356 but the effect of the 'upset' price was to increase the average (though less than the 1993 average of £854) to its 1991 and 1992 level of £788.

Top price of 5,000 guineas was received for Keith Smart's home-bred four-year-old mare Bronfoel Boneddiges Mai; the 950 guineas which he paid for her dam, Pantlleinau Myfanwy, at the 1986 sale paid dividends, since he had sold her colt foal Harri to top the colt foals at the 1991 sale, had another two daughters at home and sold the dam for 2,000 guineas that day to Holland! Two Derwen mares, both daughters of Derwen Railway Express, were next in line, Derwen Queen of the Isles went to Broughton Stud for 4,400 guineas and ten-year-old Derwen Today went

Bronfoel Boneddiges Mai, top of the 1994 sale at 5,000 guineas. Photo by Wynne Davies.

BELOW *Babiog Hedfanwr, top male at 3,400 guineas, 1994 sale. Photo by Wynne Davies.*

to Germany for 4,100 guineas, fortunately leaving three good daughters behind at Ffald Stud. The filly foal, Ffoslas Lady Model, sold for 4,200 guineas which was the second-highest foal price. Top of the males at 3,400 guineas was the two-year-old colt Babiog Hedfanwr bought by Mr Harry Johnson who bought other top Cobs the following year only to disperse them at the 1997 sale.

The 'upset' price at the 1995 Royal Welsh Sale was altered to £300 on fillies but £200 on colts and percentage sold reduced to 60 per cent, sale total down to £360, and average down to £715. This was the first time that a section C pony of Cob-type had sold for a higher figure than the Cobs; she was the filly foal Dyrfal Red Rose, which sold for 4,500 guineas. Top Cob at 4,000 guineas was the three-year-old Abergavenny Welsh Model sired by Pennal Calon Lan, the top colt foal at the 1988 sale

BELOW *Fronarth Lady's Delight, 1995 sale sold for twice as much as any other filly foal (3,500 guineas) to the USA.*

when bought by Abergavenny Stud. The top male at 2,600 guineas was the colt foal, Pennal Confidence, half-brother to Calon Lan. The top filly foal at 3,500 guineas went to the United States – Fronarth Lady's Delight bought by Thalia Gentzel, who had previously bred only section As and Bs.

Part-breds and geldings were firmly established as 'performance animals', on the first day the gelding Cascob Cardi Llwyd sold for 2,600 guineas to Germany in 1993 and the part-bred Llansantffraed Prince for 2,000 guineas. The gelding trade kept up well in 1994 with Cefncaerfor Bruno selling to France for 2,000 guineas and Okeden True Gambler fetching 1,700 guineas in 1995. Top part-bred at 1,320 guineas in 1995 was Dolau Dairy, one of a family already making a name for themselves as 'eventers' and 'hunter trials' winners, bred by octogenarian Megan Davies at Berriew, using Cob stallions on 'heavy' mares descended from the farm Shire horses. Inaugurated in 1995 prior to the start of the Friday sale was a gelding show of youngstock which were later sold at reasonable prices.

For the 1996 and 1997 Royal Welsh Sales the numbers entered fell by approximately 100 a year, 949 in 1995, 861 in 1996 and 757 in 1997, but the average price remained surprisingly constant at £715 in 1995, £702 in 1996 and £711 in 1997.

Top price at the 1996 Royal Welsh Sale was 5,100 guineas paid for the nine-year-old black stallion Mabnesscliffe Advisor whose half-brother (same dam Hewid Wendy), Mabnesscliffe Survivor, had held the sale record of 10,400 guineas since 1988. There was a better trade in foals than in top-class brood mares with old-established studs Synod, Tynybryn and Ystrad-Dewi topping the colts (Synod Robinson at 1,500 guineas) and Pennal, Cascob, Goyallt and Parc the filly foals (Pennal Wendy at 1,400 guineas). The 'champagne' moment of the sale was when Mr and Mrs Forwood sold two three-year-old geldings Cefnbangor Duke and Everest Syniad Da for 3,000 and 2,700 guineas to P.J. Exports, geldings which they had purchased at the 1993 sale as colt foals for between 200 and 300 guineas. Mr and Mrs Forwood are well known for reaching the 'tops' with their ridden Cobs, their daughter Mrs Jane Weller and grandson William Weller having won the Royal Welsh ridden classes and Olympia (ridden Mountain and Moorland) and Wembley (Mountain and Moorland Working Hunters) many times with such well-known performers as Llanina Malgwyn, another Royal Welsh Sale foal purchase. Vashti Hasdell of the Cwmduad Stud sold the top part-bred three-year-old Cwmduad Lucky Lady for 2,200 guineas (by a Welsh part-bred out of a Welsh Cob mare); repeating the 'top part-bred' achievement the following year with the three-year-old gelding Cwmduad Murphy's Pride at 2,400 guineas bred the other way round – that is, by the Cob stallion Tyngwndwn Black Magic out of a Thoroughbred mare.

There was much excitement at the Menai Reduction Sale held on 14 September 1996, when Mabnesscliffe Survivor's 1988 auction record price of 10,400 guineas was broken when the two-year-old German-bred colt H-S Martino sold for 15,000 guineas. Martino (Menai Sparkling Magic x Wiston Morwena) had won the yearling colt class at the 1995 Royal Welsh Show; he was sold to the Larsen family of Denmark but stayed on at the Menai Stud, Llandysul, Ceredigion to be produced and shown during 1998, resulting in some outstanding achievements including championships at Aberystwyth, the Three Counties, Teifyside, Cheshire County, Ponies (UK) and Llandysul.

Top of the females that day was the eleven-year-old mare, Menai Sparkling Duchess, a well-known winner who fetched 3,400 guineas. Two filly foals, Menai Pride's Choice and Menai Lively Girl, sold for 1,200 guineas each for export to Canada.

As anticipated at the 1997 Royal Welsh Sale the 'star attraction' was Harry Johnson's seven-year-old chestnut stallion, Synod Rambo, who came so close to breaking the 1988 sale record when sold for 10,000 guineas to William Gredley of Newmarket – who had not previously owned a Welsh Cob. Rambo had been bought privately by Harry Johnson as an unhandled five-year-old, then came out the following year to win championships at major shows such as the Cheshire County, where he was also the Templeton Horse of the Year Show qualifier; his 1997 winnings included championships at Glanusk and the Royal Bath and West. Top foal at 2,600 guineas was Synod Ruby Black sired by Synod Robert Black who is half-brother to Rambo (same dam Synod Rosemary, also dam of Synod Rosary top foal at the 1987 sale).

It is a very rare occurrence to breed a cremello Cob but Mrs Joan Tysilio Jones of Dwyfor Stud bred four between 1990 and 1994 and all four appeared ridden together in the sale ring to win the 1997 sale 'champagne' moment. The top mare at 2,700 guineas was Tireinon Spring Blossom, who was bought by Sonya Mindt and Tracey Edwards of the Llangennydd Stud, Gower and who also bought another nine top mares and the six-year-old stallion Trevallion Armani (equal second-highest price with Gwynfaes Sion of 4,500 guineas). The sale was also boosted when forty-nine Cobs were bought to start a riding establishment in Germany (total exports =64). The top gelding, Paith True Bloom from Mrs Barbara Phillips, also sold for export to Pat Holmes of California, setting up a new record for a gelding of 3,000 guineas. True Bloom should prove a valuable ambassador for ridden Cobs in the United States, since his breeding at the Paith Stud goes back to the beginning of the WPCS.

Appendix 4.1

LLANARTH

	No. Cat	No. Forward	No. Sold	%	Sale Total £	Av £	Av D £
1964	64	64	36	56	3,744	104	122
1965	64						
1966	98						
1967	89	83	43	52	4,883	113	
1968	75	68	47	69	5,779	123	
1969	115	110	66	60	7,828	119	
1970	132	121	80	66	9,311	116	
1971	191	180	157	87	15,808	164	187
1972	219	206	136	66	39,505	290	
1973	298	284	225	79	58,537	260	337
1974	291	266	178	67	38,902	219	
1975	284	262	216	82	42,968	199	231
1976	344	314	237	75	46,237	195	
1977	283	265	199	75	58,327	295	316
1978	284	270	221	82	76,755	347	388
1979	297	283	225	80	82,010	364	
1980	326	314	180	57	68,187	378	375
1981	253	242	155	64	55,893	360	382
1982	171	154	81	53	22,097	272	270
1983	25 Dispersal	25	25	100	15,084	603	
1984	–						
1985	–						
1986	–						
1987	–						
1988	–						
1989	–						
1990	–						
1991	–						
1992	–						
1993	–						
1994	–						
1995	–						
1996	–						
1997	–						

ROYAL WELSH

DERWEN

No. Cat	No. Forward	No. Sold	%	Sale Total £	Av £	Av D £	No. Cat	No. Forward	No. Sold	Sale Total£	Av £
–											
–											
–											
–											
–											
–											
–											
–											
–											
–											
–											
396 (Sections A, B, C & D)											
306 (Sections A, B, C, D)											
143	136	101	74	18,942	187	206					
162	141	116	82	35,795	311	369					
325	300	216	72	62,055	287						
400	345	241	70	66,176	274	298	–				
348	309	238	77	74,035	311	336	32		32	25,632	801
409	336	261	78	82,252	300	317	113		67		
420	377	276	73	86,388	313		138		77	19,305	250
437 (2 Days)	389	297	76	118,800	400		–				
600	521	364	69	132,216	363						
580	511	360	70	125,659	349						
476	402	310	77	156,463	504						
551	473	384	81	225,000	586						
634	546	453	83	358,200	791						
918 (3 Days)	796	582	73	531,027	912						
970	865	657	76	512,419	870						
865	797	584	73	460,827	789						
926	835	608	73	518,876	853						
996	885	563	64	443,356	788						
949	843	504	60	360,360	715						
861	772	477	62	334,790	702						
757	660	469	71	333,055	711						

Appendix 4.2

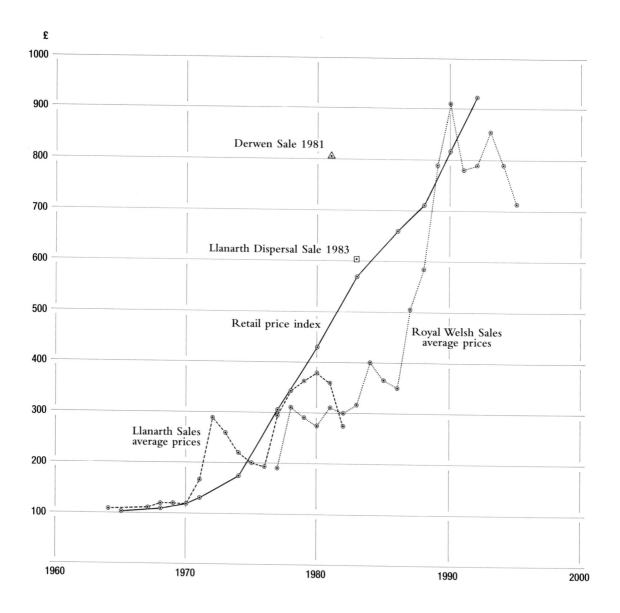

£

Derwen Sale 1981

Llanarth Dispersal Sale 1983

Retail price index

Royal Welsh Sales
average prices

Llanarth Sales
average prices

CHAPTER FIVE

The Welsh Cob overseas

WELSH COBS HAVE been imported into many countries, sometimes by the government of the country (for example, into Spain) in order to improve the indigenous native breeds or otherwise bred in a pure state (for example in the United States) where they are capable of holding their own against all the fashionable breeds from other countries. The enormous expense involved in flying Cobs to such countries as Australia and the United States of America in the late nineties has been no deterrent; obviously they are being appreciated for their conformation, beauty, versatility and ability to perform and excel in so many different disciplines.

Argentine

Welsh Cobs are not bred as such in the Argentine but stallions are imported periodically to cross with the native breeds to produce gaucho ponies. Brenin Cymru (foaled in 1925: Mathrafal Brenin x Seren Ceulan) and Mathrafal Comet (foaled in 1924: Vyrnwy Idloes x Poll of Cyffin) were imported by Sidney Poels of Buenos Aires in 1929. These two were around 14 hands in height; future imports were bigger stallions: Hercws Welsh Comet (foaled in 1941: Llethi Valiant x Teify of Hercws) in 1946 and the 15-hand Pistill Goldflake (foaled in 1941: Paith Flyer II x Pistill Nance) in 1955.

Australia

Many Welsh ponies and Cobs were exported to Australia in the nineteenth century suffering what must have been a very tortuous and long journey by convict ships from London; there was no Suez canal until 1856. A five-year-old Welsh pony stallion was advertised for sale by auction in Sydney on 18 July 1839.

The value of the Welsh Cob was appreciated by Australian 'station' owners – that is, farmers with vast acreages, also by city tradesmen who wanted smart vanners for delivery purposes; many were used by the 'Anthony Hordern Emporium' in Sydney (Anthony Hordern, CBE, was father of Lady Creswick, who set up a United Kingdom auction record when buying Coed Coch Bari for 21,000 guineas in 1978). Welsh Cobs of pre-Stud Book times appear in the pedigrees as some of the most influential Australian Stock horses and 'Walers' which were exported in vast numbers to India and the Middle East as remounts.

Vero, a bay Cob stallion bred by Evan Jones, Manoravon, Llandeilo in 1902 was owned three years later by Fell and Hogan of Melbourne; he was sired by King Flyer, (foaled in 1881) 'Ceffyl Morgan y Gors', whose sire was Welsh Flyer, foaled in 1861. Bill Price Jones (son of Evan Jones) would take ship-loads of stallions (ponies, Cobs, Hackneys and Shires) and Shorthorn bulls to Australia to sell by auction; one such stallion was Greylight, bought by Anthony Hordern for £1,000 in 1911.

Trotting Railway II, foaled in 1905 (sire of the twice Royal Welsh Prince of Wales Cup winner Mathrafal Brenin) won a second prize at Caerphilly in South Wales in 1910 and a first prize in Sydney in 1911; he was exported along with twelve mares to D. T. Davies, Mount Horeb Stud, Grahamstown, NSW.

The first Welsh Cob stallion to stand at Retford Park (Sir Samuel Hordern) was Login Briton and he was joined in 1910 by Traveller's Joy and Moordale Flyer, both from Miss Eurgain Lort's Castellmai Stud in Caernarfon. There are many champions, for example Synod William in the United Kingdom descended from Traveller's Joy, also many in Australia. Traveller's Joy was champion in harness in Sydney in 1910, 1911 and 1912. Welsh Cob breeding in Australia received another boost in 1937 with the import of the dark chestnut stallion, Welsh Rebound (son of Ceitho Welsh Comet), by J. A. Wallace of Melbourne from Mrs Lloyd and Sons of Capel Dewi, Llandysul.

Exports of ponies to Australia increased exponentially in the seventies: ten in 1972, sixty in 1974, 102 in 1976, 115 in 1978 and then settled down at about ten a year. The same period also experienced an increased interest in Cobs, starting with the stallions Brenin Pur (Rhosfarch Frenin x Lin by Brenin Gwalia, foaled in 1968) to Mrs Alison Chipperfield, Victoria; Derwen Serenllys (Derwen Rosina's Last x Derwen Seren by Coedllys Stardust, foaled in 1973) to Mrs Willsallen, New South Wales; Gerrig Arwyn (Hewid Cardi x Hewid Melda by Derwen Black Magic, foaled in 1974) who became a good harness winner for K. Hvirf of New South Wales; Gwibedog Sportsman (Derwen Llwynog x Gwibedog Daffodil by Honyton Michael ap Braint, foaled in 1974) to Dr and Mrs Myers of Victoria; Llanarth Jack Flash (Nebo Black Magic x Llanarth Flying Saucer by Llanarth Braint, foaled in 1976) to Mark Bullen and he was my choice for supreme championship when I judged there in 1985 and finally Redwood Derw (Derwen Deryn Du x Felin Tywysoges by Pentre Eiddwen Comet, foaled in 1974) to T. and B. Peel of New South Wales. Dr Myers also bought the mares Trefaes Charm and Trefaes Cymraes and started breeding good stock by Gwibedog Sportsman in 1978. Mrs Chipperfield imported Rhydlas Ramona, Mrs Sue Walsh imported Trichrug Lili and Synod Georgie Girl and I sold Saltmarsh Amanda to Mrs Goldfinch of Tasmania who later also bought the stallion Sydenham Hawfinch and mare Trevallion Bluebella. So Australia had its first big influx of outside blood since the turn of the century and classes at shows became quite respectable in terms of numbers and Australians began to appreciate Welsh Cobs for their versatility.

John and Carole Riley who established the Cwmkaren Stud in Wales in 1970 emigrated to Queensland in 1993 and in 1994 imported two Cob foals from the Nebo Stud: the colt Nebo Dyfrig Express (Derwen Desert Express x Nebo Princess Alice) and the filly Nebo Miss Wales (Ilar Bouncing Boy x Tyngwndwn Welsh Lady). Dyfrig Express is a valuable outcross and was used on four mares in 1996, all of which were found to be in foal. There were a few other Cobs to go to Australia in 1993 such as Helen Duke (Western Australia) who imported Llanarth Empress.

Belgium

The Belgisch Welsh Pony Stemboek Society is a medium-sized organisation of 240 members (1994), which by 1994 had registered 1,020 stallions, 1,310 mares, and 210 geldings in all four sections plus part-breds (section K). Exports to Belgium restarted after the war with the section D Margaret Gwenog (foaled in 1951, Llwynog-y-Garth x

Eirlys Gwenog) in 1956 to Louis van Pyperseel of Brussels. Then during the sixties, exports to Belgium were confined to sections A and B, starting with Coed Coch Samlet to Miss Babelle de Moerkerke in 1957. The section Ds were given a good boost in 1973 when Jos Ducatelle of Oudenaarde acquired the two yearling fillies Rhystyd Morwena (Rhosfarch Frenin x Rhystyd Lady Model) and Rhystyd Sunrise (Tyhen Comet x Rhystyd Bouncing Lady) and these produced influential foals in the late seventies and eighties by Trefaes Goldcrest and Rhandir Robin. Between 1985 and 1993 ten more section D stallions were imported from the United Kingdom along with thirty-two mares, also some stallions and mares imported from other countries, mainly Holland. Among the most influential stallions were Avonvalley Billy Smart, Brimstone Diplomat, Bucklesham Legend, Craigyparc King Flyer, Esceifiog Bonheddwr, Navestock William and Pentrefelin Tally Bach.

The most successful show mare in Belgium was Cascob Delight (foaled in 1982 and imported in 1983, Nebo Dafydd x Cascob Favourite). Her owner Walter von Kerschaerer brought her back to the Royal Welsh Show in 1990 where she won the section D harness class.

Cascob Delight at the 1990 Royal Welsh Show.

She also produced excellent stock such as Ring Roger, foaled in 1991, sired by Tireve Tywysog Du. She was retired from the show ring in 1995. By 1996, sixty-one section D males and 137 females have been registered with the Belgisch Welsh Pony Stamboek Society.

Canada

There are just over 300 members of the Welsh Pony and Cob Society of Canada, about 200 animals of all sections are registered annually; 6,600 animals were registered in total up to 1990 and it was estimated that there were 103 registered section Ds in Canada in 1996.

The Cobs got off to a good start in 1975 with the import of Llanarth Maldwyn ap Braint (foaled in 1974), one of the famous full-brothers and sisters by Llanarth Braint x Rhosfarch Morwena, which include the multi-champion (foaled in 1969), Llanarth Meredith ap Braint. Maldwyn was imported by Mr Thomas Isfryn Davies (a Welsh-speaking Welshman) of the Cedar Spring Ranch, British Columbia. Mr Davies later imported three Llanarth fillies, which had a great impact on Cob breeding in Canada under his 'Brynarian' prefix. The champion driving animal when I judged in Vancouver in 1995 was Brynarian Bleddyn (Llanarth Maldwyn ap Braint x Llanarth Dilys), driven by Tina Knott for his owners Sandy and Norm Evans.

Brynarian Bleddyn, driven by Tina Knott. Photo by Norm Evans.

An older full-brother, Llanarth Math ap Braint (foaled in 1970), went to the other side of Canada (Mr R. J. Nuth of Ontario) in 1976 and he has sired some good stock, among them Ardmore Todmorden. Jenny and Keith Pasons' Coblynau Stud in Ontario is led by their senior stallion Derwen Reality. The well-known harness stallion Kentchurch Rustler (Llanarth True Briton x Llanarth Rhalou) is owned by Mrs Mary Cork who also has a top-class mare Penrhyn Gwendoline, bred by Mrs Hope Ingersoll of Massachussetts, sired by Llanarth Trustful out of Gweneth Pres y Penrhyn. Two 1993 progeny of the outstanding sire Pennal Calon Lan which went to Miss Anne-Marie Morton and Mr Lawrence Flaska are the colt Abergavenny Joel out of Cledlyn Ladybird by Geraint Brynawelon and Ceulan Caitlan out of Coediog Catrin by Penlluwch Dafydd.

Czech Republic

Reports of the outstanding qualities of Welsh Cobs reached the Czech Republic in the late nineties, with some Czech horse breeders attending the October 1997 sales where they purchased Rhystyd Stepping Model, Glantraeth Welsh Maid, Glantraeth Welsh Charm, Hendrewen Hannah and Gerrig Rebecca. These represented some valuable bloodlines from old-established studs and will be a good foundation for the Welsh Cob studs of the future in that country.

Denmark

Welsh mountain ponies were exported to Denmark in considerable numbers since 1959 but Welsh Cob breeding began in 1973 when the pioneers Joe and Lene Pearson imported some from the Scole Stud – the stallion Scole Model being an excellent ambassador with his equable temperament and performance abilities. The next Danish stallion was Dyfnog Valiant (by Derwen Rosina's Last) imported by Danish Welsh Pony and Cob Society chairman Marianne Seidenfaden, who also bought several good mares. Marianne is a leading driving expert and soon had her Cobs and their progeny competing against the best in harness competitions. She later imported the experienced event driving stallion, Parc Brigadier (who held the record Sale price of 3,000 guineas at the Llanarth Sale in 1980 until 1987: Talley Wendy), and in 1994 another stallion, Menai Sparkling Omega.

Through the eighties Cob numbers in Denmark increased slowly but consistently – for example good mares came from Trefaes, Twyford, Scole, Kentchurch and Parc Studs but also stallions such as Derwen Arthur got the Cob breeding going in Jutland. Since the late eighties Cob breeding in Denmark has become more popular and breeders who previously concentrated on their Welsh ponies have now diverted their interests to Cobs; the most successful Stud in this period has been the Valhalla Stud (Carl Trock and Karen Olsen) which was founded on two Rotherdale mares and the stallion Calerux Black Prince. This Stud, with these three animals and their offspring, won the Danish Supreme Championships at all the DWPCS gradings since 1987 and one of the offspring is Valhallas Emily, champion Welsh Cob over many entries from the United Kingdom and seven other countries at the 1994 International Show, held in Switzerland.

More recent imports (Bent Olesen) are the two mares Nebo Cymraes and Tireve Empress and the stallions Nebo Crusader and Synod Rembrandt, the latter being the only stallion to have beaten Black Prince to date. A milestone in Welsh Cob breeding in Denmark was achieved in 1994 when Preben Russell and family secured the noted sire Parc Reveller.

Falkland Islands

Welsh Cob stallions were introduced periodically to cross with the native stock, such as the stallion Brenin Cardi (f. 1944; Meiarth Royal Eiddwen x Oakford Flash) exported from Mr Dill Thomas, Grange Stud, Neath to Mr Robert Blake, Holmstead, Hill Cove in October 1948. The Cob stallion Rhystyd Ifan-Ho (f. 1980; Geler, Ifan-Ho x Rhystyd Lively Maid) and five Cob mares Colfa Jet, Foryd Hafwen, Penwith Poppy, Plwmp Bess and Wildham Trottie True were exported in 1984 to replenish the native stock after the Falklands war.

Finland

Exports of Welsh ponies and Cobs to Finland represent the greatest promotional success of any country with all of them going via the Derwen International Centre. Whilst there were zero exports to Finland from 1901 to 1989, figures since then have been 1990:35; 1991:25;

1992:4; 1993:16; 1994:24; 1995:16. Of the thirty-five ponies and Cobs exported in 1990, ten mares and all fourteen geldings were Cobs and all thirty-five went to Mrs Kirsi Lehtonen of Littoinen. The Cob mares included Degla Princess Maid, Hewid Bronwen and Rhystyd Rhamant and the geldings Derwen Tudor King, Fronarth Brenin, Llanarth Duke and Synod Rosco. These Cobs were used for riding and driving and proved very popular so the 1991 imports included breeding stock with the Cob stallion Derwen Timekeeper, all twenty-five ponies and Cobs again going to Mrs Lehtonen. Of the four exported in 1992, two were Cob mares Derwen Tahiti and Seren Olau. Interest increased again for 1993, 1994 and 1995 with three Cob geldings and six Cob mares out of a total of sixteen in 1993, eight geldings and five mares in 1994 and seven geldings and the good mares Derwen Gwawr and Blaenpennal April Moon and the stallion Derwen Queens Counsel ensuring the production of Welsh Cobs of the highest calibre in Finland in the future.

Already by the 1995 show, animals bred in Finland were giving their imported ancestors a good run for their money, the Finnish-bred youngstock champion Kotimaen Regent being the three-year-old son of Rhystyd Rhamant sired by Derwen Timekeeper.

France

Welsh Cob breeding began in France with the acquisition in 1968 of the stallion Chiverstone Jasper (foaled in 1967: Llanarth Brummel x Risca Pearl) and the mares Granby Ramona (foaled in 1966: Llanarth Brummel x Faelog Friendly) and Isllyn Lass (foaled in 1959: Nebo Valiant x Creuddyn Alwena). Three stallions which have had a big influence on the breed are Llanarth Marc ap Braint (imported from Holland in 1970), Llanarth Fidel and Trefaes Bach, all of whom are now dead (1996). The top-priced (1,500 guineas) colt foal Sydenham Asquith at the 1993 October sales is now owned by Etienne Stevens of Tully and should prove a good outcross. Four French-bred Welsh Cobs were champions at the 1995 Shows: at Bordeaux it was La Bree (Llanarth Marc ap Braint x Granby Rosetta), at Vichy it was Roxone Cherauds (Hwylog Sensation x Hussy Cherauds) whose daughter Elan Barrade by Ceulan Nathan was reserve champion with Riga Lyndon (Twyford Duke x Lignate by Honyton Ariel) champion at the National Show.

Germany

Exports of Welsh ponies and Cobs to Germany became big business in the sixties (1961:1; 1963:16; 1964:35; 1966:107; 1972:257; compared with sixty nine in 1995) and the Interessengemeinschaft was set up in 1975 by about seventy breeders to control registrations which previously, as a federal republic, had been assigned to the Agricultural State authorities of the individual countries. There were still not too many females offered for sale, for example at the Llanarth Sales, and Welsh Cob exports to Germany began with stallions, the first being Redwood Solomon (foaled in 1967: Llanarth Braint x Derwen Black Nymph) purchased by Herr Kern (the first member to own stallions of all four sections in Germany), Teify Royal (imported into Germany after a very successful sojourn in Holland), the first German Welsh Cob champion Rhandir Tywysog Dafydd and Llanarth Morhys (Herr Otto). The first mare was the Dutch-bred Roukuilens Domitia (familie Tschoepke).

The first German National Welsh Show was held in 1976 with the largest population of Cobs coming from the countries of Rhineland-Palatinate, Westphalia, Hannover and Schleswig-Holstein. The IG-Welsh of Germany were also the first to organise International Welsh Shows (at Baden-Baden in 1978 and 1979). The two Studs who dominated the Welsh Cob scene in those days were Palatinate Stud (Herr and Frau Schmitt) and Bimberg (Herr and Frau Hueggenberg). The stallion Hewid Lyn (f. 1975 Llanarth Meredith ap Braint x Chancerie Polly) of the Palatinate Stud was three times supreme champion of the National Shows and also of the 1979 International Show; he was later joined by Parc Romeo (f. 1983: Parc Sir Ivor x Parc Judith) and the mare Trevallion Mandy's Bright Girl who later produced four National Supreme champions. The best-known of the progeny of Bright Girl (sired by Parc Romeo) is Palatinate Rose who became the first overseas-bred Welsh Cob ever to win a prize at the Royal Welsh Show (third in 1992) also she was adult champion at the 1994 International Show (Switzerland). The stallions for the Bimberg Stud were Bimberg Boyo by Bucklesham Brenin Bach and Zeus of Stowell by Oakhatch Rhyddid.

Germany has become the biggest importer of Welsh Cobs from the WPCS sales in recent years starting with ten from the 1979 Llanarth Sale and keeping up well with twenty-eight from the 1995 October sale and fifteen from the 1996 Spring sale. Owing to their versatility

ABOVE *Palatinate Rose.*

H S Martino. Photo by Eberhard Holin.

(performance classes were added to the German National Show in 1993), Welsh Cobs are now dispersed also throughout Eastern Germany, totalling about forty stallions and 400 mares and youngstock in 1996. It was a great distinction for the HS Stud of Herr Spiekermann to breed and produce the first prize yearling colt HS Martino by Menai Sparkling Magic at the 1995 Royal Welsh Show; he sold for the world-record auction price of 15,000 guineas at the Menai Sale on 14 September 1996 and was second out of thirty-three entries at the 1997 Royal Welsh Show. He sadly died in Demark in July 1998.

Holland

The two export peak figures world-wide of 1,599 in 1966 and 1,933 in 1972 were due largely to section A exports to Holland (1302/1599 and 1403/1933). The first section D imports were the two full-brothers Tywysog-y-Garth (foaled in 1960) and Brenin-y-Garth (foaled in 1962: (Brenin-y-Bryniau x Derby III) in 1963 to Mr van de Berg of Wolfheze. The mare, Wiston Welsh Maid (foaled in 1955: Brenin Gwalia x Brynarth Snip), arrived in Holland in 1965 and in 1966 the first Dutch-bred section D was born and he was named Boschveld Aladin. Tydi Pride (foaled in 1964: Llanarth Meteor x Valiant Queenie) went to Holland in 1966 to be joined by Tydi Flower Girl (foaled in 1965: Cymro Lan x Valiant Queenie) and Sawel Dorina (also foaled in 1965: Dewi King Flyer x Sawel Aures) brought by Mr Klomp at the 1967 Llanarth Sale. At the 1968 Llanarth Sale Mr Visser bought Pink Glancie and Mr Klomp bought the top colt Teify Royal and the mare Arthen Amanda. Arthen Amanda later went to Mr de Later to be foundation mare of his Emmickhovens Stud producing e.g. the brothers Emmickhovens Valiant (f. 1980) and Amor (f. 1984), sired by Nebo Comet out of Emmickhovens Rapid, daughter of Arthen Amanda and sired by Rouwkuilens Freedom (Teify Royal x Tydi Flower Girl). Also in 1968 the Royal Welsh winner, Llanarth Marc ap Braint, was exported to Mr Joop Poldervaart but he was sold on to France in 1970 when Mr Poldervaart suffered an accident. Mr Poldervaart however retained his interest in Welsh Cobs and when he recovered, bought Llanarth Shon Cwilt (prizewinner at the Three Counties and Royal Agricultural Society of England Shows) after the 1975 Llanarth Sale from Mr Nelson Smith.

By 1969 there were sufficient Welsh Cobs in Holland to hold classes for them at shows and they turned up in large numbers at the first show at Deurne. At the 1984 International show held at Ermelo, the champion was Berkswell Eirlys, daughter of Arthen Eirlys (owned by Mr Huggenberg of West Germany); she was followed in her class by the two Dutch-bred, Emmickhovens Padilla and Emmickhovens Rapid, both daughters of Arthen Amanda and owned by Mr de Later. Another very successful champion mare was Hirfryn Lynwen (f. 1974: Llanarth Flying Comet x Hendre Tanwen) exported to Miss Astrid Markus in 1978.

Currently there are round about 1,000 section Ds in Holland, the stallions imported from the United Kingdom up to 1990 including Bucklesham Brenin Bach (f. 1975: Derwen Black Magic x Maelog Marian), Degla Country Flyer (f. 1983: Parc Welsh Flyer x Degla Golden Rose), Derwen Prince Charming (f. 1985: Derwen Replica x Derwen Princess), Fronarth Telynor (f. 1985: Cyttir Telynor x Fronarth

Hirfryn Lynwen and Sheadon Mahogany driven by Astrid Markus.

Brenhines), Glantraeth Trysor (f. 1985: Derwen Telynor x Glantraeth Miss Magic), Hendrewen Prince (f. 1981: Derwen Rosina's Last x Hendrewen Queen), Langarth Gwnfor (f. 1974: Tyhen Comet x Langarth Gwyneth) and Nebo Sportsman (f. 1977: Nebo Brenin x Tyngwndwn Mathrafal Lady). Nebo Comet (f. 1975: Parc Welsh Flyer x Nebo Beauty) went to Holland in 1977, returned to Wales for two years then went back to Holland in 1982. British judges who go to Holland are all very impressed with the high standards there.

New Zealand

The first record of a Welsh Cob in New Zealand was in the NZ Farmer Stock and Station Journal 1916 when Welsh Meteor was advertised at stud and some of his descendants are recorded in volume I of the New Zealand Pony Register. In 1925, Mr Tom Carruthers of Otago imported the stallion, Grove Welsh Dragon, originally registered as Llwyn Comet, foaled in 1911, sired by Llwyn Planet out of Llwyn Flashlight (no relation of Llwyn Flashlight II who won the George Prince of Wales Cup at the 1911 Royal Welsh Show). With the stallion, Tom Carruthers also bought the two mares: Noyaddwilym Gwen (foaled in 1915, sired by Pride of Briton out of Black Bess by Comet Bach-Gogerddan foaled in 1891) and Hawthorne Lillie foaled in 1918, another daughter of Pride of Briton and out of Rhosfarket Favourite by Cardigan Comet III. Both were in foal to Ceitho Welsh Comet, Gwen duly produced Ghamrhiw who was to become very influential in New Zealand Welsh Cob breeding; there was no further record of Hawthorne Lillie or any of her offspring. Mr Carruthers required an outcross mare after the second war and I remember arranging the export of Llwynpiod Maid (foaled in 1944, daughter of Meiarth Royal Eiddwen) which was delayed to the end of 1948 and sadly, Mr Carruthers died before she arrived in New Zealand. However, Maid was bred from in New Zealand, her daughter by Ghamrhiw being registered as Highlay Lady.

Oakford Welsh Flyer, foaled in 1936, sired by Gwenog Welsh Flyer out of Oakford Black Bess by Ceitho Welsh Comet was re-registered in volume 32 of the WSB as Lloyd George and exported to D. D. Stewart of Wairoa in 1939. In 1971 Ron Hawker imported the top stallion Hewid Dafydd, foaled in 1965 by the top sire Cahn Dafydd out of the champion mare Chancerie Polly. Mr Hawker then obtained the mare Broughton

Alan McLachan with Ghamrhiw (in NZ) foaled in 1926.

Gay Girl (Cream Bank x Cathedine Gwlith) in 1976 but unfortunately he was plagued by ill health and bequeathed both to the WPCS of New Zealand. They were leased out to breeders and produced some very creditable progeny before Hewid Dafydd went to Australia to end his days.

Most recent imports of stallions were Bolgoed (S) Merry Madog in 1978 and Llanina Morning Blaze in 1980. Honorary life-membership of the WPCS was conferred upon Mrs Priscilla B. Neill of Otago in recognition of her outstanding contribution to Welsh Cob breeding in New Zealand.

Pakistan

Two Cob stallions were exported to the Government of Pakistan in 1952 to sire part-breds there rather than produce pure-breds. They were Deinol Welsh Comet (f. 1946: Hercws Welsh Comet x Deinol Bloss) from T. J. Jones and Son of Glynarthen, Llandysul, and Derwen Welsh Comet (f. 1947: Cahn Dafydd x Dewi Rosina) from Mr Roscoe Lloyd, Derwen Stud, Llanwrda.

South Africa

Over the years there had been a trickle of Welsh Cobs exported to South Africa but they were mainly to cross with the native breeds rather than to produce pure-bred offspring. An early example was Myrtle Gentleman, a 15-hand chestnut road stallion, foaled in 1899, sired by Trustful out of Dolly by Cardigan Comet II (foaled in 1877) which was exported to J. K. Hill, Schultz House, Monument Road, Bloemfontein in 1908. Two mares were imported by Andrew Heiddie, Table Farm, District Boshoff, Orange Free State in 1913 but there was no record of any of their progeny; they were Cerdin Bess a 15.2hh chestnut mare, foaled in 1908, bred by William Thomas, Faerdrefach, Llandysul, sired by Flying Fox out of Cerdin Beauty by Cerdin Briton (foaled in 1896) and Welsh Loo Loo another 15.2hh chestnut mare, foaled in 1907, bred by Timothy Davies, Penlannoeth, Gorsgoch, Llanybyther and sired by Old Cribon Flyer out of Penlan Bess by Flying Fox.

Interest in the Welsh breeds was renewed when Mrs Lasbrey of Cape Province imported the section A stallion, Coed Coch Seryddwr (sire of the great Coed Coch Madog), and four mares in 1948, followed by the section B stallion, Valiant to Miss Ida Illingworth Forsyte Stud, Transvaal in 1956. Numbers increased considerably in the fifties, warranting the setting up of a Society whose secretary was Miss Noel Wight of Forsyte Stud. Another big importer at this time was Mr Myburgh Streicher, who started off with three black section A mares and the black stallion, Tywysog O'Gwalia, but he soon realised that the forage of Cape Province was too rich for section As and, after importing and breeding 50 to 100 more by his next import, the very successful sire Coed Coch Nerog, turned his attention to Cobs, which created great interest among other enthusiasts. The original imports (Stud Book volume I up to 1982) were the stallions Sinton Gilbert (foaled in 1970: Gelert ap Braint x Faelog Flora by Caradog Llwyd), Oakhatch Flight (foaled in 1970: Pentre Eiddwen Comet x Maylord Charm by Gwenlli Merry Boy) and Persie Nimrod, foaled in 1978 and a member of a very famous family of full-brothers and sisters: Synod Ranger x Parc Nest. Mr Streicher then imported an outcross stallion, one of the tops in Britain, Penllwynuchel Taran, foaled in 1977: Oakhatch Cymydog Da x Pennard Boremai by Ffrwdlwyd Flying Childers, but unfortunately he did not live very long in South Africa. He was replaced by Parc Crusader, foaled in 1983, sired

Parc Crusader in South Africa 1992. Photo by Wynne Davies.

by the three times Royal Welsh champion, Cyttir Telynor out of the six times Royal Welsh champion Parc Rachel, and he has been a great success crossing with the progeny of Persie Nimrod out of the Bukkenburg imported mares, Fronarth Gwenllian and Pennal Lady May. Hewid Cymdoges Dda (foaled in 1978: Oakhatch Cymydog Da x Chancerie Polly) was imported by the Kallista Stud in 1983 in foal to Derwen Adventure Boy and duly produced a very smart filly, Kallista Rosemary, and the foundations of Cob Studs in South Africa were laid, using the best of British bloodlines. For their pioneering work, honorary life memberships of the WPCS were conferred upon Mr Streicher and the late Miss Illingworth. Greatest interest with the Welsh breeds centres on harness prowess and ponies and Cobs often compete in teams of eight harnessed to a large 'gambo'.

Spain

This is another country where Welsh Cob blood was introduced by Government officials to cross with native stock. The officials attended the 1956 Lampeter Show and selected the 1954 Royal Welsh Show Male champion Meiarth King Flyer (f. 1949: Pant Grey Prince x Meiarth Welsh Maid), for which they paid £500.

Sweden

There has been a steady trickle of section A and B ponies to Sweden since the 1959 Coed Coch Reduction Sale when Mrs Svinhufvud and Mrs Kuvlenstierna bought the two stallions, Snowdon Blighter (A) and Rhydyfelin Selwyn (B), and four mares. Photographs of their A and B champions since 1974 appear in the booklet produced by the Svenska Welshponnyföreningen. It was only in 1987 that the Stud Book was opened for section Ds after the purchase of Derwen Tennessee Express by Gunn Johansson of the Burhults Stud who had seen him winning the foal class at foot of his dam Derwen Tawela (reserve champion) at the 1986 International Show at Aachen. Tennessee Express returned to compete at the 1990 International Show at Roskilde, Denmark and in 1992 at Peterborough where he was fourth in hand and third under saddle against the best in Britain.

Before stallions and mares are accepted for the Stud Book, they have to pass an inspection for type, conformation, progeny and performance; Derwen Romeo (older than Tennessee Express) has the distinction of section D registration number 1 and by 1996 there were nine licensed stallions and forty-one mares in the Stud Book which, with their progeny, total about 200 Welsh Cobs in Sweden. The champion Cobs have been 1988: Derwen Sioned, 1989 and 1990: Cippyn Red Repeater, 1991: Cippyn Red Crusader, 1992 and 1995: Derwen Tennessee Express, 1993: Hafael Jan and 1994: Derwen Thora. In 1992 and 1993 Tennessee Express and Hafael Jan were Overall supreme champions over all the Welsh breeds. By now Swedish-bred stallions have been awarded licences – for example, Burhults Junior (Tennessee Express x Hafael Jan) and Burhults Black Commence (Tennessee Express x Derwen Sioned).

Switzerland

There is no Welsh Pony and Cob Society as such in Switzerland but an overall National Society of 1,200 members overseeing several breeds: Connemaras, Dartmoors, Fjords, Mazedonier, New Forests, Shetlands,

Derwen Tennessee Express ridden by Gunn Johansson. Photo by Eva Bahr-Turndahl.

BELOW *Kentchurch Ithwen (left) ridden by Silvanna Scherrer; Lockeridge Tabitha ridden by Andi Gattiker; trekking in the Swiss mountains. Photo by Wynne Davies.*

Spotted horses/ponies, Swiss riding ponies and the four Welsh sections and part-breds. The major breeders are Mrs Esther Hofer, Chalfont Stud (member of the WPCS since 1977) and Miss Petra Donath Platinarth Stud whose Studs are based on Maesyrafon Caryl and Derwen Dylanwad (Chalfont) and Lockeridge Tabitha and Kentchurch Ithwen (Platinarth). The foundation Stud stallion at Platinarth was Palatinate Llewellyn bred at Hermann and Ursula Schmitt's Palatinate Stud in Germany. History was made at the 1992 International Show (held at Peterborough) when the three-year-old dun filly Platinarth Fidelity (Palatinate Llewellyn x Kentchurch Ithwen) bred in Switzerland came to compete in the United Kingdom and she stood fourth in a very large class.

The United States of America

Welsh ponies were exported to the United States as early as the 1880s but the WPCS of America was not established until 1907 and then interest dropped during the depression years. One of the earlier Cobs to be exported to the United States was Temptation, foaled in 1909, bred by John Thomas of Tre'rddol (my grandfather's uncle) who won championships at both the Royal Agricultural Society of England and Royal Welsh Shows in 1914 and went to W. H. Millspaugh of Ohio and later Mr Simpson of Aurora in 1915. Mathrafal Broadcast (foaled in 1926) was sold from Criban Stud to Mrs Alice McLean of Long Island, New York in December 1937 but this lady died in a year or two and there was no trace of where the stallion went or any of his progeny. The import of section A ponies into the United States reached an all-time high of 650 in 1957 but there was no mechanism available for the registration of Cobs in the United States. Mrs Hope Garland Ingersoll had been breeding Welsh ponies at Buzzards Bay since 1914 and, having bought her first Cob mare Nebo Fair Lady (foaled in 1961: Meiarth Royal Eiddwen x Tyngwndwn Mathrafal Lady) in 1965, Mrs Ingersoll started up her own Cob registry within the American WPCS. In 1968 Mrs Ingersoll increased her Cob Stud with the imports of the stallion, Turkdean Sword Dance, and the mares, Llanarth Dancing Satellite and Llanarth Phillida, and again in 1986 with the mares, Okeden Welsh Princess, Pennal Mattie, Rhystyd Fancy and Synod Rosie O'Grady and the stallion Llanarth Trustful in 1987. For her outstanding contribution to Welsh Cob breeding in the States Mrs Ingersoll was elected to

Nebo Fair Lady (left) and her daughter Fair Tegolin of Penrhyn.

Honorary Life Membership of the WPCS. To date 34,000 Welsh ponies and Cobs have been registered within the Welsh Pony and Cob Society of America Stud Book, which adopted Mrs Ingersoll's register in the seventies. Of the 34,000 approximately 1,000 are Cobs.

Probably the best stallions currently in the United States are Nesscliffe Sunrise (Mabnesscliffe Survivor x Tireinon Dawn), Minyffordd Megastar (Minyffordd Dictator x Beech-Hay Dairy Maid), Parc Dilwyn (Parc Boneddwr x Parc Annabell), Kentchurch Chime (Parc Commando x Llanarth Rhuddel) and Derwen Denmark (Derwen Rosina's Last x Derwen Dameg).

The stallions which have had the greatest influence are Dafydd y Brenin Cymraeg (bred by Mrs Ingersoll Parc Dafydd x Llanarth Dancing Satellite), owned by Carlene Sharples of Windcrest Farm, Cascob Flying Colours (Nebo Dafydd x Cascob Mary Ann) and Derwen Rebound (Derwen Rosina's Last x Derwen Rosie), both owned by Gordon Heard

of Crossroads Farm and Mrs Ingersoll's Turkdean Sword Dance. Winks Prophesy of Penrhyn (Dafydd y Brenin Cymraeg x Nebo Fair Lady) and Dai Hanesydd Y Penrhyn (Dafydd y Brenin Cymraeg x Llanarth Phillida), both bred by Mrs Ingersoll and owned by the Winkelman family are probably the most prolific since the Winkelmans have a large Stud farm. Dafydd y Brenin Cymraeg and Turkdean Sword Dance both died in 1995. Cob numbers had their greatest boost in the early eighties with imports of between ten and fifteen per year, which are substantial numbers considering the high cost of flying them out.

In Switzerland: (from left) Chalfont Black Knight (Martina Konzler), Fatima v Gruntal (Gioia Schwarzenbach), Kentchurch Ithwen (Michelle Toloffi), Chalfont Caradog (Michelle Albrecht). Photo by Wynne Davies.

CHAPTER SIX

Performance

THE PERFORMING prowess of Welsh Cobs has been a source of great pride to breeders for centuries – stallion owners would challenge other owners to trotting races along the main roads. Their fame had spread outside the Principality, Roy Charlton admitting in his book, *A Lifetime with Ponies*, that Comet had improved the Dales and Fell breeds in Northumberland in the 1860s and recording that he had trotted ten miles in thirty-three minutes carrying a twelve-stone man on his back. Chapter 1 also contains many references to the stamina of the Welsh Cob such as the one who was the sole finisher at Badminton hunt at the turn of the century. The demands made upon the Cob in different areas also influenced their development e.g. the Breconshire Cob was used mainly for shepherding and hunt, favouring a more 'rangy' type of Cob with a good 'front', sloping shoulder and long striding movement, a typical example being the 15-hand Pistill Goldflake (foaled in 1941), who was exported to the Argentine. Cardiganshire Cobs were required more for farm work, the favoured type being smaller, thick-set with more upright shoulders resulting in 'harness'-type action. The Breconshire-bred Llanarth Goldcrest (son of Pistill Goldflake, foaled in 1945) did not find much favour with the Cardiganshire breeders nor initially did his son, the noted Llanarth Braint (foaled in 1948) whose dam Llanarth Kilda was by the germane 'Cardi' Cob Cardi Llwyd; Braint resembling Goldflake with his long, free low stride more than Cardi Llwyd who electrified the Cardiganshire crowds with his high action.

In north Pembrokeshire since the formation of the Welsh Stud Book a big 'roadster' type of Cob had developed, indeed volume 17 of the WSB had a separate section for five stallions and thirty-two mares, all over 16 hands and all the property of the Pembrokeshire Pack Horse or Roadster Breeding Society and foaled in the years 1900 to 1913. Descended from these large Cobs were the Madeni Cobs bred by the late Mr Thomas of Pantyrodyn, Newcastle Emlyn, a typical example being the 15.2hh stallion Madeni Welsh Comet, foaled in 1955 who ended his days at the Maesmynach Stud, where he was very influential. The Maesmynach Stud currently stand five stallions, Maesmynach Cymro Coch, Maesmynach Viking Warrior, Maesmynach King Flyer, Maesmynach Welsh Flyer and Maesmynach Llwynog, all standing at nearly 16 hands and making a name for themselves as sires of top 'performers'. Viking Warrior won the 1997 British Horse Foundation's prize for the stallion of any breed siring progeny winning the most prize money for showjumping, one of his progeny Mister Woppit (part-bred registered name being Penlanganol Jasper) himself having won £3,867. Good performers usually follow in families, the well-known jumping stallion Cascob Druid (WPCS Performance Competition section D champion 1985) being the sire of Master Copperfield, winner of Open Ridden Cob classes under the aegis of the British Show Hack, Cob and Riding Horse Association.

Cascob Druid ridden by Mrs Turner, champion section D in the WPCS Performance Competition 1985. Photo: WPCS Calendar.

Master Copperfield (son of Cascob Druid) winner of championships in ridden Cob competitions. Photo by Equestrian Services Thorney.

Individual studs have developed their own specialisms, with buyers pinpointing possible sources according to their requirements e.g. Nebo, Horeb, Thorneyside for harness Cobs and Kentchurch (based on Llanarth), and Derwen for riding Cobs. Sheadon Rowan, a grandson of Llanarth Valiants Image, was successful over many years at both pony club and senior levels, in eventing, cross country for tetrathlon, and dressage. A prizewinner at preliminary, novice and elementary level dressage, he progressed to working at medium level. In the pictures he is shown as a ten-year-old competing at a BHS one-day event at Chelsworth, and at the Oakley West Pony Club Senior Tetrathlon, where he was always clear and successful in Senior Tetrathlon competitions over a period of four years.

When FEI Combined Driving started in the United Kingdom, the Welsh Cob was the natural choice for many competitive drivers. George Bowman, Britain's top FEI whip started winning with his team of Welsh Cobs in the early seventies. His team, comprising Cathedine Welsh King, Courtneys Tawny Boy, Madeni Spitfire and Nebo Tywysog, won the

ABOVE *Louise Halsall riding Sheadon Rowan, grandson of Llanarth Valiants Image, at a BHS one-day event at Chelsworth in 1994. Photo by Anthony Reynolds LBIPP, LMPA.*

Louise Halsall riding Sheadon Rowan at the Oakley West Pony Club Senior Tetrathlon.

Nebo Tywysog, Cathedine Welsh King, Courtneys Tawney Boy and Madeni Spitfire driven by Mr Collinson. Photo by Sally Anne Thompson (WPCS Calendar).

Gieves National Championship in 1974 and were awarded the WPCS Brodrick Memorial trophy for this outstanding achievement in 1975. This team was later sold to Alan Bristow and driven by Mr Collinson to further successes.

George Bowman put together another team which included Scole Zircon and his half-brother Scole Jade bred by the 1990 WPCS President Mrs Gladys Dale. George Bowman won the National title twelve times in sixteen years and the International Grand Prix for the tenth time in 1996 more recently with 'Cumberland' part-bred Cobs but Scole Zircon was a member of his team in the World Championships in Holland in 1976 and Hungary in 1978 when the British team won the bronze medal. Zircon was a key member of the Bowman team until 1982 when he became a member of John Richards' team in two further World championships: Hungary in 1984 and Ascot in 1986. Another enthusiast who has had considerable success with his Welsh Cobs in FEI Team driving is Alwyn Holder from Surrey. He was a member of the gold medal-winning British team and finished in fourth place individually in the 1980 World Championships at Windsor. With the quality which shines in the show ring, coupled with the strength and stamina shown in the hunting field, the Welsh Cob is unbeatable in all three phases of the

Driving Trials. Their natural exuberant action assists them in dressage, their strength and power makes light work of the cross country while their intelligence and agility get them through the hazards. The Fosse Manor Hotel's Cwrtmynys Bleddyn and Caigers Golden Nugget have been very successful in Pair competitions and Carol Boswell, driving her mother's (Gladys Dale) Scole Andrew and Scole Jubilee, have been equally successful in tandem. Welsh Cobs outclass the other native breeds in Private Driving competitions and Tradesmen's Turnouts, a carry-over from the times when they were bought in their hundreds to deliver milk and newspapers in the large English cities. There were record entries at the 25th Annual British Driving Society at Smiths Lawn in 1989 and the

ABOVE *Scole Jubilee and Scole Andrew driven by Carol Boswell. Photo by Alf Baker (WPCS Calendar).*

Cwrtmynys Bleddyn and Caigers Golden Nugget. Photo by Ronni Nienstedt (WPCS Calendar).

Concours d'Elegance was won by a handsome chestnut Cob Rhystyd Dafydd driven to a Lawton Round Back gig. Despite the popularity of their own native breeds, Welsh Cobs are often preferred in overseas countries e.g. Milos Welde, the Austrian National Driving champion's favourite drive was his home-bred Welsh Cob Geschwendt Roving Fellow, whom he drove regularly in the heaviest traffic through city centres. As might be expected the fiercely contested private driving classes at the Royal Welsh Show are dominated by Welsh Cobs. Winners featured here are (single) Welsh Cob stallion, Lakeside Bionic Bill, driven by Mrs Aileen Booth and the pair of mares (half-sisters) Nesscliffe Jewel and Nesscliffe Tanya driven by Mrs Bridget Wessely and the passenger is the breeder Mr Frank Roberts of the Nesscliffe Stud.

The Misses Taylor and Saunders-Davies of the Llanarth Stud were probably the first to appreciate that the enormous natural extension in some strains of Welsh Cobs was ideally suited to dressage; they had the extension without the need of being trained. For harness competitions, Cobs would be trained with heavy shoes and tight side-reins in the way

Lakeside Bionic Bill driven by Aileen Booth. Photo by Anthony Booth.

that the Llanarth Stud presented the five-times Royal Welsh Show champion Llanarth Flying Comet. However, in the Llanarth Braint 'Breconshire' strain, they had an un-tapped source of natural extension at the trot which was unknown outside the Principality and created great interest when the Llanarth ladies presented Llanarth Braint to the English dressage community.

It was during the seventies and eighties that Welsh Cobs proved their worth in dressage competitions, the stallion Hewid Meredith (foaled in 1974) ridden by Laura Vintcent representing Britain at the European Dressage Championships, Söder, Germany in 1984 and another stallion Scole Cam (also foaled in 1974) was winning dressage competitions until twenty years old. The answer to their success lies in their bloodlines, the Llanarth Braint families with sloping shoulders, equable temperaments and in-bred intelligence. Hewid Meredith was sired by Llanarth Braint's son, Llanarth Meredith ap Braint of the same era as Llanarth Flying Comet, but as different as chalk and cheese. Scole Cam was sired by Scole Morhys by Llanarth Rhys, a stallion renowned for his prowess in the hunting field; Scole Cam's dam was Bisley Dafydd's Cariad, daughter of Granby Rebecca by Llanarth Brummel by Llanarth Braint.

Welsh Cobs are noted for their kind temperaments, yet they are immensely intelligent and always willing and fearless. Ten Cobs who had never met one another before, were trained in two days to perform a spectacular display at the 1984 Horse of the Year Show, a display which culminated in them all jumping through hoops of fire.

When Welsh Cobs compete in Open Ridden Cob classes under the rules of the British Show Hack, Cob and Riding Horse Association they are often not credited with their registered WPCS names and parentage. This is a great loss to the WPCS and an injustice to the breeders. One of the most successful ridden Cobs of recent years is 'Tom Cobbley' whose WPCS name is Oughtrington Monarch, sired by Trevallion Warlock out of Bolgoed Honor and bred by Laurie Harrison of Lymm, Cheshire.

The ridden Welsh Cob classes at the Royal Welsh Show, where all entries have to be shown under their registered names reached unmanageable numbers by 1995 and had to be split into separate classes for stallions, mares and geldings and even then attracted the following numbers of entries: thirty-five stallions, fifty mares and thirty-four geldings. This is the fastest growing section within the Royal Welsh Show – for instance by 1997 with similar numbers of stallion and mare

ABOVE *Nesscliffe Jewel and Nesscliffe Tanya driven by Mrs Bridget Wessely with passenger Mr Frank Roberts (breeder of Jewel and Tanya).*

Hewid Meredith ridden by Laura Vintcent at the European Dressage Championship Söder, Germany in 1984.

Scole Cam ridden by Julie Hugo, 2nd in the Medium Dressage Shell Gas Regional championships in 1992.

Tom Cobbley (Oughtrington Monarch) overall ridden cob champion, Shropshire and West Midland Show, 1996.

entries the gelding figure had increased to forty-two and plans are now afoot to further sub-divide the classes into age groups. Every animal is ridden by one judge and a second judge gives marks (usually 50:50) for conformation/type. The ride judge at the 1995 Royal Welsh Show was International Event rider Mrs Mary King. Ridden Welsh Cob classes are equally popular outside the Principality e.g. 1997 entries were twenty-eight at the Royal of England, thirty-three at the Royal Bath and West and fifty-nine at Northleach.

The jumping ability of the Welsh Cob has been well documented for four centuries, Tudur Aled a Welsh poet of the early sixteenth century wrote:

> Neidiwr dros afon ydoedd, Naid yr iwrch rhag y neidr oedd;
> Wynebai a fynnai fo, Pe'r trawst, ef a'i praw trosto.

> He was a jumper of rivers, His jump was like that of a   roebuck
>   from a snake;
> He would face anything he wished, Even if it were a roof-beam,
>   he would attempt to clear it.

With showjumping having become so professional and so exacting, the place of the pure Welsh Cob in such competition has been largely taken

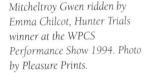

Mitcheltroy Gwen ridden by Emma Chilcot, Hunter Trials winner at the WPCS Performance Show 1994. Photo by Pleasure Prints.

over by Welsh Cob part-breds (chapter 8) where many are unsurpassed, but the pure-bred is still often to the fore in Hunter Trials and in great demand for the hunting field.

Welsh Cobs have carried the shepherds over the Welsh mountains for centuries; the 1989 President of the WPCS Mr Mostyn Isaac regularly rode his 1967 Royal Welsh Champion stallion, Honyton Michael ap Braint, shepherding over the Manmoel mountains until the stallion was

Honyton Michael ap Braint ridden by 1989 WPCS President Mr Mostyn Isaac. Photo by David Lewis.

thirty years old, often his sheep-dog (as in this photograph) also enjoyed the ride! With the advent of four-wheel cycles, there is less demand for four-legged shepherd-carriers but there are still some terrains inaccessible to the cycle. The loss of trade for shepherding has more than been taken by the trekkers, some trekking centres keeping 100 to 150 Welsh Cobs, mainly bought at the October sales and lent out to families for the winter months.

The WPCS Publicity Committee runs a Performance Points competition with points awarded varying from 500 to the winner of a 100-miles long distance ride or a BHS Two/Three Day Event to fifty points to the winner of a Private Drive or a ridden Show class. The Supreme champion over all the Welsh Breeds and Part-Breds usually collects between 7,000 and 11,000 points apart from a record 14,535 won by section B Towy Valley Corniche in 1993. The Welsh Cob stallion, Kentchurch Commandant (for combined Training), was the first to achieve 10,000 points (10,490 in 1982) to be supreme champion, the other section D supreme champion being the showjumper Parclletis Glyndwr with 9,295 points in 1992; he was also reserve supreme with

Brynymor Comet ridden by Anne Loriston Clarke. Photo by Brooke Photographic.

7,505 points in 1991. The champion Cobs have often been driving animals e.g. Scole Nora who amassed over 5,000 points every year between 1986 and 1989 and the stallion Calerux Boneddwr topped the section with 5,686 points in 1995. Brynymor Comet, ridden by Anne Loriston Clarke and driven by his owner Mr John Holmes, was top in 1980 and 1981. Hunter trial Welsh Cobs have also fared well, Cascob Druid winning in 1985, Trevallion Cadno winning in 1983 and Ruxley Merlyn being reserve supreme to Parclletis Glyndwr in 1991. Llanina Malgwyn, winner of the section with 6,050 points in 1994, 7,335 points in 1996 and 6,800 points in 1997, is a very well-known working Hunter pony winner and has often held his own against all the other native breed qualifiers at Wembley and Olympia, winning the Wembley championships in 1996 and 1998.

Ruxley Merlyn ridden by Roy Wilmin, champion at the WPCS Performance Shows in 1994 and 1997. Photo by Pleasure Prints.

CHAPTER SEVEN

Influential studs

Large numbers of studs have had an important influence on the Welsh Cob breed and it has been difficult to select a representative sample for this publication. Profiles of some thirty studs were prepared but the space available has limited the number to ten studs from Wales and three from England as being representative. The final selection is based on studs which have bred Royal Welsh Show champions, either in hand, driven or ridden. Other major studs, such as Ebbw and Tireinon, are included in the chapter on the stud on which they were based, in this case Cathedine. Some studs, such as Synod and Menai, which were considered to be predominantly section C, have been omitted, but are, of course, no less important.

Berkswell Trevallion

The Trevallion Stud owned by Mr Nelson Smith and family of Kenilworth Road, Balsall Common, West Midlands, with between twenty and twenty-five section D brood mares is the largest Welsh Cob breeding establishment outside Wales and probably ranks amongst the largest three or four in the world. Nelson's grandfather, Wisdom Smith, had been a buyer of Cobs for the Cavalry in World War I and Nelson's father, also named Nelson, preferred a Welsh Cob to any other breed for driving in busy city traffic. Nelson junior, however, bred Appaloosa horses but in 1967 his father told him that he was setting off to Cardiganshire to buy a Welsh Cob filly and that was the start of the Trevallion Stud, originally registered under the 'Berkswell' prefix and, as the Welsh Cob numbers increased, the Appaloosas were gradually dispersed.

After visiting several Cardiganshire Studs, Nelson Smith senior finally settled on a dun two-year-old filly with four white legs, Arthen Eirlys from the stud of Mrs Davies and Son of Rhiwarthen, Capel Bangor, Aberystwyth; Mrs Davies's in-laws, the Williams Brothers of Cynnullmawr, Llandre were well-known breeders and exhibitors of Welsh ponies and Cobs in the early days of the WPCS.

Arthen Eirlys was sired by the dun 1955 Royal Welsh winner Caradog Llwyd out of Patsy by Brenin Gwalia; Patsy hailed from a long line of Cobs bred by the Humphreys family of Cwmcoy, Blaenpennal, her dam Scot being sired by Vyrnwy Flyer and Scot's dam Derby II by Trotting Jack (foaled in 1908).

Athen Eirlys lived up to expectations and there could have been no better foundation for the Stud, firstly producing Berkswell Bluebell (1970), Black Tulip (1971), Eirlys (1972) and the colt Cream Jack (1973) all sired by one of Nelson Smith's first favourite stallions Tyngwndwn Cream Boy who stood at Stud with Mr Eddie Price at Marlow. Before Mr Smith purchased his own stallions, Eirlys then produced Trevallion Eirlys by Llanarth Braint in 1974, later progeny being by Trevallion Stud's own Tyhen Comet (Trevallion Anwen in 1975), Cippyn Real Magic (Trevallion Black Diamond in 1977) and Derwen Telynor (Trevallion Trotting Jack in 1978). Her 1977 foal, Trevallion Black Diamond, was the first of the 'Trevallions' to take the show ring by storm, winning at Lampeter, the Royal Welsh and the female championship at the Royal Agriculture Society of England Show; she also made her mark on the export trade, her colt foal Trevallion Comet's Last (the last foal of the great Tyhen Comet) being exported to Australia. The reason for the change of prefix from Berkswell to Trevallion was that the WPCS decided in 1974 that every breeder's prefix had to be registered and Miss Hallmark-Smith of Penrhiwllan, Llandysul got in first and registered 'Berkswell' so from 1974 Mr Nelson Smith's Cobs have been registered under the prefix 'Trevallion'.

Another 'Arthen' Cob mare to be added in 1973 (as a one week-old foal) was the dark bay Arthen Bernadette sired by Llanarth Meredith ap Braint out of Arthen Perl (Perl like Arthen Eirlys being a daughter of Patsy) and Bernadette won first prize in the youngstock class at the 1974 Royal Agricultural Society of England Show against two and three-year-olds. Bernadette produced Trevallion Mark by Tyhen Comet in 1976 and Trevallion Monty by Cippyn Real Magic in 1977 and was sold to Mr

Griff Jenkins (lot 98) for 1,100 guineas at the 1977 Llanarth Sale in foal to Derwen Telynor. The resulting foal for Mr Jenkins, named Cyttir Telynor was sold as a foal (380 guineas) to the Fronarth Stud and is the only living stallion to have twice won the George Prince of Wales Cup at the Royal Welsh Show (1982 and 1987) and he topped the WPCS sire ratings in 1985. Nelson Smith soon regretted selling Bernadette and bought her back on Mr Jenkins's death in 1979 and she has continued to breed exceptional stock at Trevallion. Another original mare to have a profound influence on the Trevallion Stud was Parc Ormond Jolly II (foaled in 1963, sired by Pentre Eiddwen Comet out of Parc Duchess, daughter of Parc Lady); Jolly II won a second prize at the 1974 Royal Agricultural Society of England Show, she was dam of Berkswell Beauty and later Trevallion Telynor. Gornoeth Cindy (Nebo Black Magic x Gornoeth Rosie) was the highest-priced filly when bought at the 1974 Llanarth Sale; her full-sister Gornoeth Candy had also topped the Sale the previous year. Another influential mare was Faelog Fashion, dam of the full-brothers many-times champions Trevallion Kojak Comet (f.1975) and Trevallion Prince Comet (f.1977), a noted sire in South Wales e.g. of the 1994 Royal Welsh winner Abercippyn Rose Cariad, who was also supreme champion of the 1997 and 1998 Northleach Shows.

The breeding mares between about 1975 and 1980 were nearly all based on Pentre Eiddwen Comet bloodlines and included: Rhandir Rachel and Rhandir Rhiannon, Paddock Rosinda and Paddock Sian, Hewid Linda, Geler Eirlys who topped the 1973 Llanarth Sale, Valiant Dandy, Parc Mandy, Gerrig Brenhines, Dilys Golden Glitter, Trefaes Ceridwen, Tyhen Topsy, Nantcol Flying Lady and Nantcol Party Girl, Aberaeron Nans Merch Sian, Rhydlas Shoned, Fronarth Blodwen, Nebo Welsh Lady, Creuddyn Susan and Jenny Llinos-y-Gored, quite a variety of bloodlines that were tried to see which crossed most successfully with the Trevallion stallions.

An obviously successful breeding mare was Tapton Rachel (foaled in 1976) sired by the Trevallion Stud's Derwen Telynor out of Tyhen Princess, daughter of the wonderful matron Tyhen Mattie (George Prince of Wales Cup winner in 1962). Rachel when mated to Cippyn Real Magic in 1981 produced Trevallion Pearl, one of the most successful of the Trevallion Show mares, she was champion at Northleach in 1991 and the National Pony Society Show in 1994 and dam of the brilliant 1997 Royal Welsh champion Trevallion Giorgio foaled in 1991 and sired by Brynymor Welsh Magic. The stallions have already been quoted, they were selected with the utmost care. Nelson Smith was very impressed with the 1973 Royal Welsh champion, Nebo Black Magic, and enquired from the Derwen Stud whether he was for sale. Magic was not for sale but at Derwen was a very promising yearling colt by Magic (and he was bought and named Derwen Telynor) out of Derwen Seren Teledu ('TV star', so named since she appeared on television as a foal with her dam, the 1968 Royal Welsh champion Derwen Rosina). Telynor has left a whole host of lovely daughters at Trevallion, passing away in August 1995.

Trevallion Pearl, champion at Northleach 1991. Photo by Wynne Davies.

By the time the 1968 Royal Welsh champion Tyhen Comet was acquired, he had suffered badly with chronic laminitis but, with the great care and attention offered to him at Trevallion, he lived on until 1988, again leaving a big mark on the breed in general, not only at Trevallion.

Trevallion Giorgio, Overall Champion at the 1997 Royal Welsh Show. Photo by Janneke de Rade.

Arthen Bernadette had won the youngstock championship for Trevallion as a two-year-old at Lampeter in 1975; the two-year-old colt class had been won by Derwen Stud's Brynymor Welsh Magic with Mr W. Ll. Rowlands's Cippyn Red Flyer second. Red Flyer was another which Nelson Smith tried to buy but again he was not for sale. His yearling black full-brother, Cippyn Real Magic, was bought instead and what a wise purchase he proved to be! Real Magic could always be relied upon to put up a great show. By 1992 most of the females at Trevallion were related to him and he was sold to Mr David Edwards of Abercippyn Stud, who had long been a supporter and taken many visiting mares to him.

Brynymor Welsh Magic was leased for 1989 and one of his sons, Trevallion Spartacus, now holds court at Trevallion along with Trevallion President Dino, son of Tapton Rachel. Rachel's daughter Rhoda is dam of the 1995 North Wales premium stallion Trevallion Can Comet and Trevallion Valentino now at Danaway Stud where Danaway FlashJack (another Rachel g-son) was Glanusk youngstock champion in 1995 and their senior stallion Trevallion Harry (f. 1986) was Northleach champion in both 1990 and 1995.

Trevallion Cobs have many times topped the October Sales, going on to have great influence throughout Britain; they have also won most major awards culminating in the ultimate dream of every breeder to win

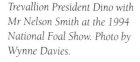

Trevallion President Dino with Mr Nelson Smith at the 1994 National Foal Show. Photo by Wynne Davies.

the Prince of Wales Cup at the Royal Welsh Show which they succeeded in doing in 1997 after thirty years. Mr and Mrs Smith have four daughters and eight grandchildren to guide the Trevallion Stud into the next century.

Blaenwaun, Gwarffynnon, Bryn Arth, Horeb

The first three prefixes may not be household names because very few mares were kept, but the Rees family deserves a chapter in any Welsh Cob history as a dedication to their devotion as stallion owners, which was uninterrupted for 120 years. Starting with Thomas Rees (1862–1951), this family clung tenaciously to the 'Cob of Old Welsh stamp' as engraved on the Prince of Wales Cup, and beat the alien infiltrators, against fashionable trends. For the first eighty years they 'travelled' their stallions along lonely, plodding miles, despite the vagaries of weather, clinging with dedication to the breed and strain started by Thomas Rees in the eighteen seventies, with the stallions often covering between 150 and 200 mares each. Their livelihood depended on their judgement of their stallions; the stud fees were the only source of income to rear large families.

Thomas Rees first began travelling stallions in Glamorgan and Monmouth in 1876 when he was barely fourteen years old; this was with the stallion Britonian who, of course, lived in pre-Stud Book times. When volume I of the Welsh Stud Book was published in 1902, Welsh Cobs were divided into two sections: 'C' for Cobs over 13.2hh and under 14.2hh and 'D' for Cobs over 14.2hh. There were ten stallions in section C of which six were pure Hackneys. The twelve stallions in section D were all of Welsh descent, two of them, Briton Comet (foaled in 1893) and King Briton (foaled in 1889), were owned by Thomas Rees, who then resided at Cwmgwenin, Llangeitho. Both stallions traced back to tap-root sires, Fanny, g-dam of Briton Comet was by True Briton and Doll, dam of King Briton was by Cymro Llwyd. Another of the twelve was High Stepping Gambler (foaled in 1984), owned by Thomas Rees's brother-in-law Evan Davies, Penrhiw, Silian who exported him while still in his youth to Bloemfontein, South Africa. All three stallions were sired by Welsh Briton, who was Thomas Rees's first stallion. High Stepping Gambler was 15hh, Briton Comet and King Briton were 15.2hh and Welsh Briton 15.3hh.

Thomas Rees had three sons, the eldest of whom, Harry (born in 1888), travelled stallions for his father until his untimely death in 1931. The other sons were James (1890–1965) and David (1892–1969). James Rees's first 'season' was in 1907 with King Briton in Glamorgan and his last in 1963, with Meiarth Royal Eiddwen. In between he had Blaenwaun Artful Briton (by Briton Comet), Blaenwaun True Briton (foaled in 1922 by High Stepping Gambler), Blaenwaun King Briton (foaled in 1932 by Blaenwaun True Briton out of Blaenwaun Flora Temple, champion mare at the 1929 Royal Welsh Show) and Gwarffynon Artful Briton (foaled in 1948) by Blaenwaun King Briton.

David Rees's first stallion was High Stepping Gambler II (foaled in 1902 and died in 1934) who won sixty-five first prizes (John Roderick Rees has a leather girth with medals engraved with these prizes) and of course, the George Prince of Wales Cup in 1909. The 1919 Royal Agricultural Society of England Show was held in Cardiff and High Stepping Gambler II was again champion. It was in 1908 that he became the property of David Rees and he served over 100 mares every year (187 in 1917) at £2 Stud fee and 2/6 groom's fee, the income boosted by the £100 premium award by the War Office. One of his foals was Blaenwaun Flora Temple (bred by Thomas Rees in 1923), who was champion mare at the 1929 Royal Welsh Show and she bred six foals by Brenin Gwalia – one of which was Bryn Arth Stepping Gambler (foaled in 1946) (g-sire of Llanarth Brummel Royal Welsh champion in 1964 and 1965), others being Bryn Arth Madonna (foaled in 1942 and she stayed on to do the farm work) and Bryn Arth Pride (foaled in 1948) from whom the champions Fronarth Boneddiges and Fronarth Welsh Model are descended. High Stepping Gambler II was also sire of Flower, dam of the noted Llethi Valiant (George Prince of Wales Cup winner in 1931) and also of David Rees's third stallion Gwalia Victor.

The second stallion was the smaller Mathrafal Brenin (foaled in 1911) sired by Trotting Railway II who was exported in 1911 to New South Wales, Australia. Mathrafal Brenin was bred by William Watkins, Beaufort, Gwent, who called him Young Railway (after his sire), then he was bought by Mr Meyrick Jones who 'baptised' him as Mathrafal Brenin. From Mathrafal he was sold to Mr F. Butler of St Albans and David Rees bought him in 1921 on Mr Butler's death for £290, a big sum for a Cardiganshire smallholder in the hungry twenties. Mathrafal Brenin won the George Prince of Wales Cup in 1924 and 1925 and died suddenly from anthrax while travelling around Breconshire in 1928. Two days before he died Mathrafal Brenin served a mare called Doll, the resulting filly, Cymraes, being dam of David's Rees's immortal Brenin Gwalia.

The third stallion, Gwalia Victor, was foaled in 1924, sired by High Stepping Gambler II when his sire was twenty-two years old and he was champion Cob at the Lampeter Shows in 1929, 1930 and 1931. When he was premium stallion for mid-Cardiganshire in 1931 he covered 128 mares. He travelled around Breconshire in 1933 covering Cymraes and subsequently Brenin Gwalia was foaled in 1934 and bought by David Rees and son John Roderick when six months old and died with them in 1965 aged thirty-one years. Brenin Gwalia was introduced to stud work when only two years old and Gwalia Victor was disabled for two weeks. During these two weeks Brenin Gwalia served sixteen mares and returned home none the worse. Twelve different judges in successive

Brenin Gwalia with Mr David Rees (1948). Photo by Farmer and Stockbreeder.

years awarded him a Cardiganshire premium and he would serve 100 to 150 mares annually until he became semi-retired in 1955, from then standing at stud at home at Bear's Hill, Penuwch, Tregaron to where David Rees and John moved in 1950. Brenin Gwalia won the stallion class at the first post-war Royal Welsh Show (1947) from such great names as Mathrafal, Meiarth Royal Eiddwen (his son), Churchill, Brenin Cardi, Pistill Gold Flake, Cahn Dafydd and Tywysog Gwalia, in that order. He was reserve to Meiarth Welsh Maid for the George Prince of Wales Cup (which she later also won in 1949, 1950 and 1954), she being by Llethi Valiant (grand-son of High Stepping Gambler II) out of Meiarth Pride by Mathrafal Brenin.

Two Royal Welsh champions sired by Brenin Gwalia are Princess (Cathedine Stud) and Rhystyd Prince (Gwenfo Stud), and he was g-sire of the further champions Geler Daisy, Honyton Michael ap Braint, Cathedine Welsh Maid, Ffoslas Flying Rocket and Porthvaynor Gold Dust. Brenin Gwalia was buried at Bear's Hill when thirty-one years old in the spot where his g-sire High Stepping Gambler II had been buried thirty-two years earlier.

Brenin Gwalia's place at John Rees's one-stallion stud was taken over by his son Rhosfarch Frenin (foaled in 1961), son of Rhosfarch Morwena, who went on from Rhosfarch to Llanarth, where she produced eleven foals by Llanarth Braint. Rhosfarch Frenin's greatest influence on the breed probably came through the Cilsane mother and daughter Morfydd (foaled in 1960 by Cahn Dafydd out of Creuddyn Megan) and her daughter Stella, foaled in 1966, sired by Churchill. Their two foals, both foaled in 1972, were Kilgour Welsh Monarch and Ebbw Prince and by a strange act of fate, both died in 1995. Kilgour Welsh Monarch fetched the highest price (1,400 guineas) at the 1982 October sales when he was purchased by John Roderick Rees's son Roderick Lloyd Rees who had by now set up his own Stud at Brynmerwydd, Horeb, Llandysul. Kilgour Welsh Monarch's greatest claim to fame is as sire of Horeb Euros winner of the George Prince of

Rhosfarch Frenin with Mr John Roderick Rees (1977). Photo by Alison Chipperfield (Australia).

Horeb Euros with Mr Rod Rees, Overall champion Royal Welsh Show 1993. Photo by Anthony Booth.

Wales Cup at the 1993 Royal Welsh Show and supreme champion at Lampeter in 1992 and 1993. Another full-brother Horeb Harry Parry (Mrs Sarah Russell, Brimstone Stud) was male champion at the 1994 Royal Agricultural Society of England Show.

Ebbw Prince has sired eight full-brothers and sisters out of Cathedine Pride II; these include Ebbw Amber Flash, who was second to Horeb Euros at the 1993 Royal Welsh Show, Ebbw Viscount, champion Cob stallion at the 1995 Lampeter Show and the forever popular Ebbw Victor, supreme champion at the 1993 Royal Agricultural Society of England Show and male champion at the Royal Welsh Show in 1983, 1984 and 1997, and finally winner of the Prince of Wales Cup at the age of 19 years in 1998. Thus the bloodlines begun by Thomas Rees in 1876 are holding their own after four generations of humans 120 years later.

Cathedine

The Cathedine Stud was started in 1941 when Mr Tom Evans bought a dark chestnut Cob filly foal for £8. This was 9604 Victory Maid, bred some twenty miles away by William Price, Tregare, Builth Wells; she was sired by the 15-hand Paith Flyer II out of the smaller Fly (foaled in 1925) by Ffynonwen Young Defiance. Paith Flyer II was of a more 'leggy' type than that favoured in his native Cardiganshire but was a popular sire in Breconshire where he sired, amongst others, the big Pistyll Goldflake, g-sire of Llanarth Braint. Paith Flyer II was sired by Vyrnwy Flyer, another big horse who was later gelded and sold to the United Dairies, spending the rest of his life on the London streets pulling milk floats. By a coincidence, Cathedine Stud's other foundation mare Wyre Star was a grand-daughter of the same Vyrnwy Flyer, though she had no connection with Breconshire and ended up at Cathedine from Llangwyryfon in Cardiganshire via Caernarfon and Llangollen! Paith Flyer II's dam Paith Trilby (foaled in 1913) was sired by the Norfolk Hackney Dilham Confidence, whom we met in chapter 1. Tom Evans bred Princess out of Victory Maid in 1949 (sired by Brenin Gwalia) before the Cathedine prefix was adopted from the name of the

Princess ridden by Mr Tom Evans, Champion Royal Welsh Show 1957. Photo by Wynne Davies.

farm in Bwlch, Brecon, where the family have lived for eighty-six years. Princess achieved her moment of glory at the Aberystwyth Royal Welsh Show in 1957 when her name was engraved onto the George Prince of Wales Cup after she beat the illustrious Parc Lady, Derwen Derwena and Tyhen Beauty in the mare class and the male champion Pentre Eiddwen Comet and reserve Llwynog-y-Garth for the championship. Princess also won the ridden Welsh Cob class in 1957, the only mare ever to have won both. By 1954 the 'Cathedine' prefix had been registered with the Welsh Pony and Cob Society and her later progeny were Cathedine Flyer (1954) by Llwynog-y-Garth, Cathedine Lady (1960) by Brenin Gwalia, Cathedine King Flyer (1962) by Verwig Mathrafal, Cathedine Victory Pride (1963) also by Verwig Mathrafal and Cathedine Rainbow (1965) by Hendy Brenin. Surprisingly this female line was not kept on at Cathedine though Cathedine Rainbow was used on Welsh Maid to produce Cathedine Pride II (Ebbw Stud) and Cathedine Victor (the 1971 son of Cathedine Victory Pride) to produce Cathedine Dewdrop (1977) which was sold to Nesscliffe Stud.

The other foundation mare Wyre Star was bred in 1944 by Dan Jones, Brynchwith, Llangwyryfon whose grandfather William Jones owned Eiddwen Flyer (foaled in 1877), she was sired by Brenin Gwalia out of Lady Wyre (foaled in 1926) who was by the aforementioned Vyrnwy Flyer out of Coedllys Pet (foaled in 1919), the Coedllys family breeding some very good Welsh Cobs until their dispersal in 1995.

Wyre Star was sold by her breeder in 1947 to Huw Owen, Is-Helen, Caernarfon who sold her on to R. T. Evans of Llandyn Hall, Llangollen, owner of the famous Mathrafal. Wyre Star produced Collen Queen and Collen Country Swell in 1950 and 1951 by Mathrafal and another two by Brenin-y-Gogledd, Collen Princess and Collen Myfanwy in 1953 and 1955.

Wyre Star at the 1954 Royal Welsh Show. Photo by Wynne Davies.

Wyre Star spent four years at Cathedine before being sold to Laurie Evans of Penally in 1961. At the Teilo Stud she produced Teilo Chocolate in 1962 by Verwig Mathrafal (a filly whom I bought in 1965 and who went on to become a very successful show jumper), Teilo Star and Teilo Pip in 1964 and 1965, both sired by Heather Royal Eiddwen. During her time at Cathedine, Wyre Star produced three daughters, two of whom were sold on, and yet she had begun a dynasty of Royal Welsh champions (the first two who were sold were also g-dams of Royal Welsh winners) at Cathedine and also progeny which have taken the sale rings by storm! First at Cathedine, Wyre Star produced in 1958 Cathedine Gwlith by Cathedine Flyer (Llwynog-y-Garth x Victory Maid); Gwlith was sold to the Broughton Stud in Aylesbury where, among others, she produced Broughton Ivy, who goes into the history books as one of only three Cob mares (the other two being Derwen Queen and Dewi Black Bees) to have produced two Royal Welsh Prince of Wales Cup winners, in Ivy's case: Ffoslas Black Lady (1979) and Ffoslas Flying Rocket (1980). Cathedine Pride, foaled in 1969, also by Cathedine Flyer was sold to Roy Higgins of the Tireinon Stud at the 1961 Hay-on-Wye Sale. Wyre Star herself died in the autumn of 1965.

The influence of Cathedine Pride has gone far and wide via the Tireinon Stud, Tireinon Dawn (foaled in 1964, sired by Llwynog-y-Garth) being dam of Glanvyrnwy Stud's top sire Nesscliffe Rainbow. The Cathedine Pride daughter to have the greatest influence was Tireinon Spring Song (foaled in 1967 by Hendy Brenin), she died in January 1991 at the age of twenty-four, having produced sixteen foals, including Tireinon Shooting Star (foaled in 1975, won the foal class at the Royal Welsh Show and was sold to Nesscliffe Stud, finally ending his days as a very successful sire at Cascob Stud), Tireinon Triple Crown (foaled in 1981, topped the 1984 Builth Sale at 2,200 guineas and won the harness class at the 1989 Royal Welsh Show), the two full-brothers and one sister Tireinon Confidence (1983), Gwenlais (1984) and Step On (1986) all sired by Derwen Railway Express and all now very important members of the Derwen Stud and finally in 1990 Tireinon Spring Blossom, top female on the 1997 Royal Welsh Sale.

The Wyre Star daughter to stay at Cathedine was Cathedine Welsh Maid, foaled in 1961 and sired by Cahn Dafydd; she was female champion of the 1970 and 1974 Royal Welsh Shows and produced twenty-three foals, fifteen of which were sired by Parc Welsh Flyer. Welsh Maid's first daughter foaled in 1965 and sired by Hendy Brenin was Cathedine Welsh Model. She won the foal class at the Royal Welsh Show and was sold to Mr Dennis Bushby as foundation for the Buckswood Stud. Welsh Maid's second daughter (foaled in 1968) was Cathedine Pride II, sired by Cathedine Rainbow, she was sold to Albert and David Weeks's Ebbw Stud, her best-known progeny being eight full-brothers and sisters by Ebbw Prince, which include the champions Ebbw Amber Flash, Ebbw Rosina, Ebbw Viscount and one which can include many victories under his belt, such as the Supreme championship of the 1994 Northleach Show and male championships of the 1983, 1984 and 1997 Royal Welsh Shows and finally the 1998 Royal Welsh Prince of Wales Cup at the age of 19, Ebbw Victor.

The first of the fifteen foals to be sired by Parc Welsh Flyer was Cathedine Maureen (foaled in 1970), who was a well-known winner (e.g. at the Royal Welsh Shows in 1970, second in 1971, first in 1977, fourth in 1981) and a wonderful producer, such as Serene (sold as a foal in 1980 for 1,000 guineas), Snow Queen (first at the 1981 Royal Welsh) and Telynor, foaled in 1984, three times youngstock champion at Lampeter for Fronarth Stud and also winner of adult classes e.g.

champion at the 1989 Aberystwyth Show. Following Maureen (in 1971) was the full-sister Cathedine Agnes who also was retained at Cathedine; she won the foal class at the Royal Welsh Show and was in the first three in the mare classes there in 1978, 1979, 1983, 1984 and 1985. We have already met Agnes's 1981 foal, Cathedine Pure Maid who twice topped the Builth Sales, firstly when she was sold as a foal then in 1988 when Mr Evans bought her back for 3,400 guineas, the other sale topper being her daughter Cathedine May Princess who sold for 3,000 guineas as a foal at the 1992 sale. Cathedine Welsh Lady, foaled in 1980, dam of the 1990 top foal Cathedine April Sunshine (3,400 guineas) is again one of the fifteen Parc Welsh Flyer x Cathedine Welsh Maid family. Welsh Lady also is a well-known show mare, her best success probably being at the 1991 Royal Welsh Show, where she stood second amongst Britain's best to the eventual female champion, Fronarth Welsh Model.

Of the eight full brothers by Parc Welsh Flyer, the three best known are Cathedine Danny Boy (foaled in 1975), Cathedine Express (foaled in 1982) and Cathedine Flying Express (foaled in 1986). Danny Boy and Express were both sold to David and Gwyn Dobbs and both won

Cathedine Flying Express with Mr Ernie Beynon. Photo by Wynne Davies.

Lampeter Show championships, Danny Boy in 1980 and Express in 1991. The Dobbs family sold Danny Boy to Mrs Julia Hoskins for whom he won many prizes under saddle before going to Mrs Jo Lutey's Trevarth Stud in Cornwall, where he has proved a very useful sire of both pure-bred and part-bred Cobs. Express was sold to Mrs Bridget Wessely, where he continued as Stud stallion also excelling under saddle and in harness before being sold for 5,000 guineas at the 1993 Builth Sale and his death the following year was a great loss to the breed in North Wales. Flying Express was sold to Miss Melita Watkins as a foal, was second out of thirty stallions at Lampeter in 1994 for the South Wales premiums and, out of sixty stallions entered for the 1991 Royal Welsh Show, Cathedine Express was awarded the fifth prize and Flying Express was sixth. This whole family are noted for their equable temperaments; I have often borrowed Flying Express for stud purposes and he was a real gentleman. We had three foals by him in 1992, one of which went to Canada.

The Cathedine Stud has had a great influence on many studs throughout Britain and Mr Tom Evans was a very worthy President of the Welsh Pony and Cob Society for 1995–6.

Derwen

The Derwen Stud was started in 1944 when Mr and Mrs Roscoe Lloyd returned from London to their native Dyfed in mid-Wales. Both families had previous connections with the WPCS. Mr Roscoe Lloyd's father was Evan Lloyd of the Pencarreg Stud at Aberaeron who kept many Cob and Hackney stallions at stud, including the well-known Hackney Thornton Chandos, bred in Lancashire in 1899. Cobs did all the farm work at Pencarreg; there is a photograph in a WPCS Journal of Roscoe Lloyd's sister Caroline riding the Cob mare Violet and there is a report of her jumping side-saddle over a six foot wall while out hunting!

Mrs Elin Lloyd's father was Daniel Jenkins, headmaster of Llanycrwys school near Llanwrda, a founder member of the WPCS, who also farmed at Pentrefelin, Talsarn. Daniel Jenkins's brother Jenkin Jenkins registered in volume I of the WSB a little mare named Nans o'r Glyn, foaled in 1891. At the time of Jenkin Jenkin's death in 1907, Nans o'r Glyn had won 217 steeplechasing and galloway races, been placed second sixty-one times, third sixteen times and only eight times unplaced. In 1944 the family lived at Garth Villa, Llanbyther, the best-known Cob to be registered under the name of 'Garth' being Llwynog-y-Garth who was bred by Mr T. E. Thomas of Llanfair Caereinon in 1944, went to Garth, was registered as a two-year-old and was sold to Mr Dilwyn Thomas of Grange Stud, Neath for whom he won the male championship at the 1949 Royal Welsh Show to be followed by the same awards in 1950 and 1960 but, despite many championships throughout Britain, never quite got his name engraved on the Royal Welsh Prince of Wales Cup.

The first Cob to be bought by Mr Roscoe Lloyd was the eleven-year-old mare Dewi Rosina, bought at Llanbyther Market in 1945 for £97, and who became the foundation of what is today the largest Welsh Cob Stud in the world. Rosina's dam was Dewi Black Bees who had won the Royal Welsh Prince of Wales trophy in 1935 and she was sired by Ceitho Welsh Comet (foaled in 1913) by Caradog Flyer by Young Caradog by Caradog by Welsh Jack by the original tap-root sire Cymro Llwyd. In 1948 the family moved to Derwenfawr Farm, Crugybar and the 'Derwen' prefix was adopted.

Every Cob currently at Derwen Stud is descended via one channel or another – some via many channels – from Dewi Rosina, Derwen Stud having concentrated on line-breeding encouraged by the successes of Pentre Eiddwen Comet (foaled in 1946), probably the most influential sire of the post-war era, who was sired by Dewi Rosina's son Eiddwen's Image out of Rosina's dam, Dewi Black Bess. Dewi Rosina won the female championship at the 1951 Royal Welsh Show, then went a stage further by winning the Prince of Wales Cup in 1953, a feat which the Derwen Stud has achieved a further eleven times, with her great-granddaughter Derwen Rosina in 1966, 1967 and 1968, with Nebo Black Magic in 1973, Derwen Rosinda in 1981, possibly the greatest of them all Derwen Princess in 1983 and 1984, Derwen Groten Goch in 1986, 1990 and 1992 and Derwen Dameg in 1989. To cap all this another Derwen mare, Derwen Viscountess (half-sister to Princess) owned by Dan Haak of the Uplands Stud, Hampshire won it in 1985, beating the Derwen Stud's own male champion, Derwen Replica.

Derwen Rosina was bought from her breeder Mr E. J. Williams as a foal in 1962, her dam Rhandir Black was a daughter of Pentre Eiddwen Comet. Derwen Rosina produced Derwen Deryn Du by Llanarth Braint, Derwen Llwynog by Nebo Black Magic (bought back to be senior sire after a period of long distance endurance riding). Derwen

*Derwen Princess, Overall
Champion at the 1983 Royal
Welsh Show. Photo by Mark
Bullen (Australia).*

Seren Teledu (Welsh for Television Star since she appeared on television
as a foal), Derwen Queen (foundation of the Princess Duchess and
Viscountess family), then in 1970 at the peak of her career she died
leaving a four-week foal, later to be named Derwen Rosina's Last, and
top the WPCS sire ratings in 1976 and equal-top with his sire Nebo
Black Magic in 1978. In 1963 the family moved to Ynyshir Farm,
Pennant, enabling the stud to expand considerably and at the first
Derwen Stud Open Day held on 8 June 1986, the five stallions were led
by twenty-five-year-old Nebo Black Magic, followed by his two sons,
the full-brothers Llwynog and Rosina's Last, Llwynog's son Derwen
Replica and Derwen Railway Express (foaled in 1977: Nebo Black
Magic x Derwen Rosie), whose progeny have sold for top prices at the
Royal Welsh Sales and won major awards qualifying the sire to occupy
high positions in the sire ratings scheme.

The twenty mares and fillies were divided into four family groups,
the first three groups descended from Derwen Rosina and the fourth
from Groten Ddu. Leading the females was the seventeen-year-old
Derwen Queen (daughter of Rosina), the originator of the Derwen
'Royal' line, she was accompanied by her dual Royal Welsh champion
daughter Derwen Princess and another daughter Duchess who,

although herself never been shown, is dam of Geler Stud's top sire Derwen Desert Express and she was accompanied by her daughter, the 1989 Royal Welsh champion, Derwen Dameg, dam of the United States champion Suzanne Glenn's Derwen Denmark and Mrs Hofer's Derwen Dylanwad, champion in Switzerland. Another Derwen Rosina daughter was Derwen Seren Teledu (dam of Trevallion Stud's famous sire Derwen Telynor); she was accompanied by her daughter Derwen Tlws, and Tlws's daughter, the 1986 International Show champion Derwen Tawela, who is herself dam of the top stallion in Sweden, Derwen Tennessee Express. The next family was headed by Derwen Rosie, g-daughter of Derwen Rosina; she is best known for her three sons, all top sires, Derwen Railway Express, Rhuban Glas and Reply. The last family figure-head was the twenty-two year-old Derwen Groten Ddu who had been bought back by Derwen Stud after a period at the Penygarreg Stud. Groten Ddu is a grand-daughter of the 1936 and 1937 Royal Welsh champion Teify of Hercws and Groten Ddu's 1981 daughter Derwen Groten Goch was Royal Welsh champion three times (1986, 1990 and 1992).

The proceeds of the 1986 Derwen Stud Open Day went towards the furnishing of the WPCS Pavilion which had just been erected on the

Derwen Groten Goch with Mr Ifor Lloyd. Photo by Wynne Davies.

Royal Welsh Showground and the Society was greatly indebted to Ifor, his wife Myfanwy and son Dyfed and other local handlers and friends as well as the Derwen Stud staff for making this such a memorable event. Indeed, the Derwen Stud 1986 Open Day had been so successful that the family was persuaded to repeat it in 1990, when again over £2,600 was raised for the WPCS, many visitors having come from overseas countries and some by their own personal helicopter! The parade again started with the families of mares; it was a glorious sight, the foals scampering around the large ring against the backdrop of Cardigan Bay. The 'Royal' family was again headed by Derwen Queen and her captivating foal King of Wales by Rosina's Last. Seren Teledu had died but her 'T' family were there in strength, led by the two full-sisters Tlws and Telynores and their daughters Tawela, Tlysni and Tegan. Derwen Rosie had also died at the good age of twenty-four years in 1987 but the 'R' family again was well represented and finally the 'Groten' family, where a much-fancied young mare was Groten Goch's five-year-old daughter, Derwen Groten Felen. Finally, for the females, twelve young fillies were paraded, showing that the future of the stud was on a very sound footing.

The stallions were represented by the twenty-eight-year-old Nebo Black Magic and his two sons, Derwen Llwynog and Rosina's Last, then Derwen Adventure Boy (Cefn Parc Boy x Brynymor Aurwen) whose stock has gone all over the world and whose United Kingdom daughters include the 1988 Royal Welsh female champion Northleach Duchess and finally in hand, Derwen Quartz, a four-year-old stallion which provided an interesting outcross since he is sired by Rhystyd Flyer (Parc Welsh Flyer x Rhystyd Lively Maid) out of Queen of Hearts. Finally, three young stallions appeared under saddle: Texas Express (Railway Express x Tegan) who was just starting Long Distance riding; Tireinon Step On, another four-year-old (Railway Express x Tireinon Spring Song by Hendy Brenin), which had been bought by Derwen Stud to introduce some more Hendy Brenin blood and, judging by his eight foals on view that day, was doing a very satisfactory job and finally another Rhystyd Flyer son, the five-year-old Derwen Two Rivers, a supreme champion under saddle who had qualified for the Bronze Buckle at Endurance Riding at his only attempt.

Again, the WPCS benefited financially with a considerable donation; Ifor and Myfanwy had been involved in months of preparation and so had the Derwen Stud staff, led by overseas enthusiasts Tovey Virkelyst and Karin Fjeldbo. The Lloyd family must be 'gluttons for punishment' and volunteered to host another Open Day on 18 June 1994 with the proceeds going to the Ceredigion RWAS Appeal Fund which is earmarked for the construction for a new stable block on the Royal Welsh showground. Enthusiasts attended from as far afield as the United States, Sweden, Finland, Canada, Switzerland, Holland, France, Denmark, Germany and all quarters of Britain. Nebo Black Magic and Derwen Llwynog were sadly missed this time, having passed away at the goodly age of twenty-nine and twenty-four, respectively in 1991 and Rosina's Last had died in 1993. The very sad absentee was the great Derwen Replica who had died a few weeks previously, but he was represented by his son, Duke of York and full-brother, Requiem.

The other stallions paraded were Derwen Two Rivers, Derwen Quartz, Derwen Adventure Boy and Tireinon Step On, who was also joined by a more recent Derwen Stud purchase, his full-brother Tireinon Confidence. To start the mares, fourteen with foals at foot were paraded individually the foals were showing off well and five found new homes that day! Then followed the sixteen mares due to foal shortly, led by the twenty-five-year-old Derwen Queen (she died in 1996) and her two famous daughters, the twenty-two-year-old Princess and twenty-one-year-old Duchess. With such a wealth of talent, it is no wonder that the Derwen International Welsh Cob Centre has exported animals to thirty-two overseas countries. The display ended with the ridden stallions, demonstrating dressage and jumping and the Royal Welsh Agricultural Show Appeal fund benefited to the tune of almost £12,000.

Mr Ifor Lloyd became Chairman of Council of the WPCS in April 1997, the seventh in ninety-six years, Mr J. J. Borthwick and The Lord Kenyon having been in office for some thirty years each: 1932–62 and 1962–91. Mr Ifor and Mrs Myfanwy Lloyd's son Dyfed Roscoe Lloyd is proving to be a very competent rider and won may prizes in 1997 riding Derwen Rosa.

Ffoslas

Welsh Cobs and Shires had been kept as work horses for many generations of the Evans family of Tylau, Bwlchllan, Lampeter and when William Evans married Eiddwen of Ffoslas, Bronant in 1952, she brought to Tylau an interest in registered Welsh Cobs, her uncle Mr D. L. Lloyd

Davies having been owner of the big winner Trotting Jack (foaled in 1908), and winner of the WPCS medal at the 1914 Welsh National Show at Newport. The last of their working Cobs, a daughter of Blaenwaun True Briton, proved difficult to breed from, so a two-year-old filly Lin was bought in 1966 and Mr Evans joined the WPCS that year.

Lin came from a long line of good Cobs bred by the Humphreys family of Cwmcoy, Blaenpennal, originating from Derby F. S. (foaled in 1908) and her daughter Derby II, foaled in 1912 and sired by Trotting Jack. Lin was sired by Brenin Gwalia and was covered by Brenin Gwalia's

Mr and Mrs W J Evans with Ffoslas Filmstar. Photo by Carol Jones.

son Rhosfarch Frenin, duly producing Brenin Pur in 1968; Brenin Pur was exported by the Hon. Mrs Kitson to Alison Chipperfield's Wingana Stud in Victoria, Australia in 1976 and he has had a marked influence on the Welsh Cob breed 'down under'. Lin later produced Ffoslas Harvest Moon by Parc Welsh Flyer in 1971, then the full-sisters, Ffoslas Linda and Marian, in 1973 and 1974 by Llanarth Meredith ap Braint. Linda went on to be a top brood mare at Heulwen Haf Jones's Foryd Stud producing amongst others the 1991 Lampeter winner Foryd Welsh Flyer. The greatest influence on the Ffoslas Stud occurred in 1970 when the four-year-old mare Broughton Ivy was purchased (lot 24) at the 1970 Llanarth Sale. Ivy was sired by Cream Bank (Tyngwndwn Cream Boy x Verwood Blodwen Bracken) out of Cathedine Gwlith (Cathedine Flyer x Wyre Star); she had bred one foal at Llanarth and went on to produce another twenty at Ffoslas.

Famous amongst Broughton Ivy's progeny are two George Prince of Wales Cup winners: Ffoslas Flying Rocket (sired by Rhosfarch Frenin, foaled in 1972) for Heulwen Haf Jones in 1980 and Ffoslas Black Lady

Ffoslas Black Lady, Overall Champion 1979 Royal Welsh Show with Mr Jack Lloyd. Photo by Carol Gilson.

(sired by Brenin Dafydd in 1973) in 1979 for Ffoslas Stud. Black Lady was always shown by Jack Lloyd, Meiarth Stud, whose father David Lloyd had been a showing rival of Lloyd Davies with Trotting Jack. Ffoslas Black Lady is the most successful show mare yet to come from Ffoslas, winning, in addition to the Prince of Wales Cup, the female championship at the 1980 Royal Agricultural Society of England Show and the barren mare class at the 1984 Royal Welsh Show. She has also been an exceptionally successful producer, her 1986 daughter Ffoslas Welsh Lady by Parc Welsh Flyer being dam of the 1994 stunning filly foal Ffoslas Lady Model by Parc Sir Ivor, who created great excitement at the October sales when, after a long battle of bidding, she sold for 4,200 guineas, the next foal price there being 2,800 guineas.

Lady Model went to Mr Frodsham's Finneyhill Stud in Derbyshire to join Ffoslas Telynores (Cathedine Telynor x Ffoslas Black Lady and top of the two-year-old fillies at 2,200 guineas at the 1989 October sales) and Ffoslas Violet (Thorneyside Flyer x Ffoslas Black Lady, fourth highest filly foal at 1,700 guineas at the 1992 sales).

One of the earlier progeny of Broughton Ivy was Ffoslas Welsh Maid, foaled in 1974, sired by Parc Welsh Flyer and died in 1994. Her son Ffoslas Sir Gwynfor (foaled in 1980 and sired by Parc Sir Ivor) was sold to the Heaton Stud in West Yorkshire and was the WPCS premium stallion for the North of England from 1986 to 1992 with the exception of 1987 when he was leased back to Ffoslas. Having won first prizes at the Royal Welsh, Lampeter, Glanusk, Cheshire County, etc., there was great interest when he was offered for sale at the 1992 October sales where Joanne McNamara-Jones paid 5,000 guineas to secure him; this being the equal top male price and second highest overall.

Ffoslas Pride, Ivy's 1976 foal, sired by Ceredigion Tywysog, has been a little 'gold-mine' for the Navestock Stud of Brentwood Essex, one of her sons being the well-known harness winner, Navestock Marksman and two of her daughters, Navestock Welsh Lady and Navestock Rosinda, were joined by Claire Willis-Burton's Pentrefelin Boneddiges to win the Royal Welsh sire progeny competition in 1991 for Navestock Stud's Nebo Prince. Broughton Ivy died in 1990 after giving birth to her last filly, Ffoslas Honeysuckle, who is already creating an impression on the breed by producing the 1995 filly, Ffoslas Miss Honey Girl, who was the third highest filly foal at the October sales, making Honeysuckle destined to carry on the dynasty which Broughton Ivy began for the Ffoslas Stud.

Fronarth

The honour of having bred the greatest number of Royal Welsh Show Welsh Cob champions falls to the Derwen Stud with thirteen champions (ten supreme) and Parc Stud with ten championships (seven supreme), but the distinction of having owned the sires of most champions (twenty-five championships with twelve supremes) falls to the Fronarth stallions Mathrafal, his son Cahn Dafydd and his son Brenin Dafydd. More recently their Cyttir Telynor has been male champion three times (overall twice) and his daughter Fronarth Boneddiges has twice been reserve female champion, her stable companion Fronarth Welsh Model winning the George Prince of Wales Cup in 1996, after being reserve twice in 1991 and 1994 and then reserve again in 1997.

Between the two wars there were some quite well-known ponies at Frongoy Farm, Pennant, Llanon in mid-Wales, one or two of whom had acquitted themselves well racing. One 12 hand 3 in mare was Fronarth Beauty; foaled in 1936 she was mated to Brenin Gwalia, producing

Fronarth Welsh Model, Overall champion Royal Welsh Show 1996. Photo by Janneke de Rade.

Fronarth Queen Bee, a short-tailed 13 hand 2 in excellent sort of pony of Cob-type. I remember holding our section A Royal Welsh champion Dinarth What Ho to cover her for ten shillings in 1951, the resulting foal, Fronarth What Ho, later winning twenty-one first prizes in harness at the Royal Welsh Show before dying in 1984 aged thirty-two years – a good return on ten shillings by any standards!

The Jones family were a wonderful team, Mr Dafydd Jones senior, who often drove Fronarth What Ho in the show waggon, and the three sons, David John (who did the in-hand showing), Brynmor and the late Isaac. The foundation of the Cob stud can truly be regarded as Brynarth Pride from which Fronarth Welsh Model, Fronarth Boneddiges, top-priced foal Fronarth Tywysoges Wendy, etc. are all descended. Brynarth Pride was foaled in 1948, one of five full-sisters bred nearby by the late Mr David Rees by Brenin Gwalia out of Blaenwaun Flora Temple, the winning mare at the 1929 Royal Welsh Show. Brynarth Pride in 1956 produced Fronarth Flora by Mathrafal and Flora was dam of the 'typey' Brenin Dafydd and g-g-g-dam of Boneddiges. In 1960, Brynath Pride produced Fronarth Lady by Cahn Dafydd and Lady is g-g-dam of both Fronarth Welsh Model and Fronarth Tywysoges Wendy.

Another influence brought into the stud in 1972 from cousin Idris Jones was the colt foal Ceredigion Tywysog by Brenin Dafydd out of Tyngwndwn Malen and he remained a much-sought-after sire until well into the nineties. Perhaps the greatest debt of gratitude owed by the Welsh Cob breed to Fronarth Stud is for rescuing the two old stallions Mathrafal and his son Cahn Dafydd in old age and making them available to Cardiganshire breeders. Surprisingly, both stallions were eighteen years old when they arrived at Frongoy, Mathrafal going on to sire Royal Welsh champions Tyhen Mattie, Pentre Rainbow and Tyngwndwn Cream Boy and Cahn Dafydd later producing Derwen Rosina, Parc Rachel, Brenin Dafydd and Cathedine Welsh Maid.

Pentre Rainbow in 1964 sired Golden Sunshine, a well-known sire for Mrs Calvert's Rowen Stud. Golden Sunshine was leased by Fronarth Stud, again at eighteen years old in 1984 and sired Fronarth Welsh Model, overall champion at the 1996 Royal Welsh Show.

The other males to have been introduced into the Fronarth Stud have come as foals; we have already heard how Cyttir Telynor was bought as a foal for 380 guineas at the 1978 Builth Sale and went on to win the George Prince of Wales Cup in 1982 and 1987. A later acquisition was

Craignant Express, bought as a foal for 750 guineas at the 1988 Royal Welsh Sale. Craignant Express is sired by the senior Craignant stallion at Oswestry, Craignant Flyer, who is also sire of the record-breaking Mabnesscliffe Survivor. Express's dam Gwrthafarn Modern Maid was bred near Fronarth at the Messrs Rowlands's Gwrthafarn Stud; she was sired by Cippyn Red Flyer and her dam by the Gwrthafarn Stud's other stallion Twyford Druid, the g-dam by Rhosfarch Frenin out of their foundation mare Rhyddod Bess. Craignant Express in the capable hands of nephew Gwyn Jones, who joined the stud to assist his uncles in 1980, soon made his presence felt in the show ring, winning first prizes in enormous classes at the Lampeter stallion shows as a yearling, two-year-old and three-year-old (the last twice also being youngstock champion) following in the footsteps of Cyttir Telynor who won at Lampeter as a yearling and his son, Cathedine Telynor (also bought by Fronarth Stud as a foal), who won at Lampeter three times as a youngster in 1985, 1986 and 1987. The Fronarth Stud has had fantastic successes with yearling fillies at Lampeter, often in classes of fifty or more. Since 1982 these have been:

1982 Fronarth Gwenllian (Ceredigion Tywysog x Fronarth Mattie by Brenin Dafydd) first and female champion, sold to South Africa.

1984 Fronarth Boneddiges (Cyttir Telynor x Fronarth Brenhines by Brenin Dafydd) first and female champion as a yearling, also repeated as a two-year-old.

1988 Fronarth Rosina (Cyttir Telynor x Fronarth Ann by Furthermoors Solomon) first and reserve female champion.

1993 Fronarth Cymraes (Thorneyside Flyer x Fronarth Brenhines by Brenin Dafydd) first and reserve female champion.

1994 Fronarth Maria (Cyttir Telynor x Pantanamlwg Princess) first and reserve female champion to the two-year-old winner Fronarth Viscountess (Ceredigion Tywysog x Fronarth Boneddiges) who was also youngstock champion in 1995, Maria being youngstock champion in 1996 and Fronarth Model Lady best female in 1997.

Already listed at the October Sales have been: Fronarth Black Diamond (top priced mare at 4,500 guineas, 1989); Fronarth Tywysoges Wendy (top filly foal at 3,000 guineas, 1993) and Fronarth Lady's Delight (top-priced filly foal at 3,500 guineas, 1995).

Gwyn is now married to Nicola, daughter of the Blaengwen Stud, their sons Dafydd born in 1992 and Sion born 1996 (the fifth generation at Fronarth) are already showing a great interest in the ponies and Cobs, ensuring the future of the Stud into the next century.

Geler

Prior to John Lloyd moving to Facwn Farm, Llangwyryfon, in 1946 from Gilfach Farm, Llangeler, he was well known throughout Ceredigion, Carmarthen and Pembrokeshire for the Shire stallions which he travelled. This move coincided with the demise of Shire horses working on the mid-Wales farms and he bought a Cob filly to later become a breeding and working mare. Geler Bess (foaled in 1947) was bought from neighbouring farmer, Evan Williams, Rhandir Uchaf, she being sired by Brenin Gwalia out of Bess by Llethi Valiant, whom we have already met as the winner of the Prince of Wales Cup at the 1931 Royal Welsh Show. Bess's other claim to fame was as dam of Rhandir Black, whose three daughters by Cahn Dafydd were Derwen Rosina (foaled in 1962), Rhandir Rosina (foaled in 1963 and retained by Rhandir Stud) and Rhandir Margarita (foaled in 1965, Ystrad Dewi Stud).

Geler Bess was mated three times to Pentre Eiddwen Comet who was the North Cardiganshire travelling premium stallion of those years; she produced three fillies, the first one being sold before registration, the second being Geler Daisy (foaled in 1953) and the third Geler Queen (foaled in 1955) was sold to Mrs Evelyn Satchell, where she became foundation mare of the Oakhatch Stud, producing Oakhatch Tiara, who later produced the three good mares, Oakhatch Tywysen, Tanwen and Teiddwen Taran.

Geler Daisy remained at Vacwn all her life and her influence on the Welsh Cob breed has been profound. Her first two fillies, born in 1964 and 1966 (after King Flyer foaled in 1957), were sired by Cahn Dafydd, the first, Geler Ann, died after producing only one foal but this foal was the great Geler Neli; the second, Geler Eirlys, topped the 1973 Llanarth

Sale, going to Gerrig Stud. Two of her sons Geler Braint and Geler Tywysog ap Braint, were the first to sell for 100 guineas at the early Llanarth Sales. Geler Ifan Ho by Tyhen Comet, foaled in 1972, took the show ring by storm at a very early age, being youngstock champion and reserve overall male Royal Welsh champion to Nebo Black Magic when only a yearling; winner of a premium at Lampeter every time he competed, he was another who died at an early age, a great loss to the breed. Geler Daisy was successful in the show ring, winning prizes as a youngster – for example fourth prize for yearling colt or filly at the 1954 Royal Welsh Show. Her moment of crowning glory came at the 1964 Royal Welsh Show, where she was awarded the Female Championship by WPCS senior judge, Mr E. G. E. Griffith, who wrote: 'Deliberately I took much time and care in the judging of these classes. I was looking for Cobs, and to me a Cob is a strong, active animal on short legs, with well-shaped limbs, bone, substance and a good middlepiece. And a Cob, or any other horse or pony, must have good sloping shoulders and must have the free, forceful action which only good shoulders can give. The

Geler Ifan Ho with Mr William Lloyd.

winner, Geler Daisy, is a grand mare, wide, deep and standing on short legs – a true Cob'. The originator of the representatives now at Geler is Geler Neli the one-and-only foal of Geler Daisy's first daughter, Geler Ann. Geler Neli was sired by Tyhen Comet and foaled in 1969 and achieved what her g-dam had done in 1964, that is thirteen years later she won the female championship at the Royal Welsh Show.

Quite apart from her winnings, Geler Neli deserves a place in any Welsh Cob history on account of the outstanding stock which she produced, starting with Geler Brenhines, foaled in 1974 and sired by Llanarth Meredith ap Braint. Brenhines won the three-year-old class at the 1977 Royal Welsh Show, was first novice mare in 1978, third open mare to Derwen Rosinda and Penclose Rhian in 1981 with Oakhatch Teiddwen Taran (g-daughter of Geler Daisy) sixth and third also in 1982 to Derwen Princess and Rhystyd Fashion. Geler Rosann, the 1976 daughter of Neli by Derwen Rosina's Last was third also in 1982, but in the novice brood mare class, and by 1986 had graduated into the open class, where she stood second to Prince of Wales Cup-winner Derwen Groten Goch. Geler Enfys, sired by Cathedine Rainbow out of Neli and born in 1973, fetched the top price at the 1976 Llanarth Sale and became the foundation mare of the Glanrannell Stud. Geler Carlo, sired by Parc

Geler Brenhines with Mr John Lloyd.

Dafydd out of Neli and foaled in 1981, was the youngstock champion at the 1983 Lampeter and Royal Welsh Shows, a feat which he repeated at Glanusk in 1984. At the 1983 Royal Welsh Show, Carlo was joined by another two sons of Geler Neli to win the progeny competition, which is open to three by the same sire or three out of the same dam. While a stallion can sire hundreds of progeny from which to select the best three for this competition, a mare's progeny is restricted to twenty or so in her lifetime, therefore to beat all the progeny of many sires was all the more praiseworthy in the case of Geler Neli. The other two in this group were the three-year-old colt, Geler Cardi Flyer, sired by Oakhatch Rowan and owned by Doug Evans of Pembroke and the five-year-old Geler Guto Goch, owned by John Firth, who has been breeding good Cobs in West Yorkshire for many years.

Geler Carlo has won five premiums at Lampeter to stand at stud in mid-Wales; he was taken to Ermelo, Holland as a representative of the breed in 1984, and his stock have won many important prizes and commanded high prices at sales. Two of his progeny to have won at the Royal Welsh are Corscaron Moonlight and Gwendraeth Gwawr. He is the senior stallion currently at Geler Stud. By now the next generation occupy a significant position in Geler Stud. Geler Sali by Parc Welsh Flyer out of Geler Brenhines, foaled in 1981, won first prize and the female championship at Lampeter in 1983 and her daughter Geler Sara is a good winner too. Geler Sambo the 1983 son of Brenhines has become a sought-after sire. Amongst his progeny are Deytheur Dai, a very good performer under saddle in Wales before being exported to Lawrence Flaska of Ontario, for whom he has been Canadian Breed champion. John Lloyd, who judged the Cobs at the 1971 Royal Welsh Show, passed away in 1985 and the stud is now in the capable hands of his son William, Chairman of the WPCS Cob Committee, William's wife, Wendy, and their two children, Gerallt and Gwawr.

Kentchurch

The Kentchurch Stud, though recently established compared with some of the centuries-old Cardiganshire studs, has earned its place in any survey of the Welsh Cob breed via its fantastic successes with ridden Welsh Cobs, claiming a total of twenty-three Olympia qualifiers, eighteen were gained by five animals which are still at Kentchurch Stud.

It was in 1953 that Anne Salter bought her first un-registered Welsh section A mare for £35 to ride. When 'Silver' was outgrown, the family could not bring themselves around to parting with her so she was kept on as a brood mare but first of all had to be inspected as 'Welsh foundation stock' so Anne joined the WPCS in 1959 and the following year Kentchurch Silver FS1 was born, sired by the noted champion, Coed Coch Socyn.

The Kentchurch prefix came from Kentchurch Court near Hereford, where Anne's ancestors hid Owain Glyndwr, the last King of Wales, from the English and he married into the family of Scudamore, who still live at Kentchurch. In 1970, Anne married international racing driver Paul Vestey and decided that she would like a Welsh Cob to ride around their Manor House Farm, Alresford, Hampshire. Nearby lived Diana and Dan Haak of the Uplands Stud, which contained the good sire Parc Commando and Royal Welsh champion mare Derwen Viscountess. Kentchurch Stud could not have had a better launch than the acquisition in 1975 of the six-year-old cream mare, Llanarth Rhuddel, sired by Llanarth Meteor out of Llanarth Rachel by Llanarth Braint. Whilst the Cardiganshire diehards may not consider the Llanarth Braint type to be representative of 'the old Welsh stamp', it has much to recommend it when it comes to equable temperament and ability to perform.

In 1975, Rhuddel produced Kentchurch Commandant by Parc Commando, a stallion now standing with the Loriston Clarke family and very much in demand as a sire of performance horses. When Commandant competed himself, he had won one hundred championships before attaining the age of six years; he won 10,490 points in the 1982 WPCS Performance competition (the highest number of points ever for a section D stallion), was overall supreme champion of the competition, also winning championships in combined Training and Dressage and third for eventing. Rhuddel retired from breeding after producing the dun filly, Kentchurch Charisma, by Llanarth Welsh Warrior in 1990. She produced eleven foals at Kentchurch, names such as Catrin (cream filly, 1979 again by Parc Commando), winner of ridden classes at the Royal Agricultural Society of England and East of England Shows, qualified for Olympia four times and great hopes are now extended to her daughter, Kentchurch Chelsea, who appeared under saddle in 1996; Kentchurch Cerys (chestnut filly, 1982, by Parc Commando) qualified for Olympia four times; Kentchurch Chime (cream colt, 1983 by Parc Commando) one of the top driving animals in the United States; Kentchurch Crystal (cream filly, 1984, by Llanarth Mastermind), exported to Denmark; Kentchurch Charm (chestnut filly, 1985 by Llanarth Welsh Warrior), owned by older daughter Caroline; Kentchurch Cloud (cream colt, 1986 by Llanarth Welsh Warrior) ridden by Xanthe Barker for owner Mrs Ann Henriques, he was champion at the 1994 Olympia Mountain and Moorland championships and second in 1995; Kentchurch Chaos (brown colt by Llanarth Welsh Warrior), owned by second daughter Georgina and Kentchurch Cariad a brown filly, again by Llanarth Welsh Warrior in 1988. Rhuddel died as the result of an attack one night in 1991 and is buried at Kentchurch.

Llanarth Welsh Warrior, sired by Nebo Black Magic out of Llanarth Lady Valiant, was bought privately from the Menai Stud, is a perfect gentleman running out with his mares and twice qualified for Olympia himself – what more could one want! Llanarth Rhiangel, full-sister to Rhuddel, but a year younger, was purchased after producing the famous Llanarth Rhun. Rhun, possibly the biggest Cob ever bred at Llanarth, won under saddle at the Royal Welsh and Royal Agricultural Society of England Shows, and was champion at the Royal Highland when owned by WPCS 1990 President Mrs Gladys Dale of the Scole Stud, qualifying at the same time for the Wembley In-hand Championship. Rhiangel in the three years from 1986 to 1988 produced three fillies by Llanarth Welsh Warrior, the cream Whisper (1997 Royal Welsh ridden champion) the cream Rhapsody and the chestnut Request. Rhapsody qualified for Olympia three times ridden by Kim Roberts and Request also qualified three times, ridden by Carol Isaac, and was overall champion there in 1996. Having had so much success with Rhuddel and Rhiangel, their half-sister (by Llanarth Flying Comet) Llanarth Rhalou (foaled in 1974) was purchased from the University College of Wales (she was not included in the 1983 University College of Wales Llanarth Stud Dispersal Sale). Her 1984 filly Llanarth Rhagori was later purchased from Len Bigley and she was ridden champion at the 1989 Royal Welsh Show. In 1984 Rhalou produced the colt Kentchurch Rustler by Llanarth True Briton which I saw performing admirably in Canada in 1995. Then followed five by Llanarth Welsh Warrior: Rufus, Rosetta, Reward, Reality and Reflection.

Llanarth Miranda was another bloodline added to keep the 'Llanarth' flag flying; she is full-sister to the famous Llanarth Meredith ap Braint.

Kentchurch Whisper, winner of hunter trials and champion ridden Cob 1997 Royal Welsh Show, ridden by Alexia Page. Photo by Hoof Prints.

Her three daughters by Llanarth Welsh Warrior are Kentchurch Minerva (1987), Mirage (1990) and Mayday (1986), who was second out of forty-three brood mares at the 1995 Royal Welsh Show. Miranda is also dam of the champion dressage part-bred mare Kentchurch Masquerade. Another valuable breeding mare added was Sydenham Daphne (foaled in 1974 by

Two full-sisters: Kentchurch Request (chestnut) ridden by Mrs Carol Isaac and Kentchurch Rhapsody (cream) ridden by Mrs K Roberts. Photo by Anthony Reynolds, LBIPP, LMPA.

Sarnau Supreme Comet x Mynd Moonshine) who, in hand, won second at the Royal Welsh Show and championships at the Royal Agricultural Society of England and Northleach Shows. Her daughter, Kentchurch Dallas by Kentchurch Commander, was sold to Denmark, which Mrs Vestey regretted and so bought her back! Dallas's 1989 daughter, Kentchurch Dazzle by Llanarth Welsh Warrior, was the second highest-priced mare (3,100 guineas) at the 1995 October Sales. Kentchurch Destiny is a full-sister to Dallas; she won the Royal Welsh ridden class in 1993 and was champion at the Royal Agricultural Society of England Show in 1994 and 1994. Their full-brother Kentchurch Dynasty was also ridden champion many times and qualified for Olympia.

At the start of 1997 there are sixteen mares and two stallions at the Kentchurch Stud, so the Kentchurch ridden Cobs will keep the breed in the public eye for many years to come.

Llanarth, Tregarth

One wonders whether, in 1943 when the Misses Pauline Taylor and Barbara Saunders Davies joined the WPCS, they had any suspicion that they were laying the foundations of a world-famous breeding establishment. Pauline Taylor came to Blaenwern Farm, Llanarth, from the Music Department of the University College of North Wales, Bangor, and Barbara Saunders Davies from Paris, where she studied music with Nadia Boulanger. Miss Taylor was an accomplished cellist and, joined by Miss Enid Lewis, whose family has farmed Blaenwern for centuries, travelled throughout Wales giving thousands of school children their first experience of instrumental and chamber music. The 'Dorian Trio' was disbanded when Miss Lewis went to London to become Professor of Pianoforte at the Guildhall School of Music and Drama for twenty-six years and the Misses Taylor and Saunders Davies set out to breed Welsh Cobs, Welsh Black cattle, Welsh pigs, Llanwenog sheep and Cardigan corgis.

Their first Welsh Cob mare was Llanarth Firefly, bred by Mr Lloyd of Hengenaint, Aberaeron in 1933 and sired by Blaenwaun True Briton from a daughter of Plynlimmon Champion. One can imagine my surprise on accompanying my father to judge at the 1945 Cardigan Show, to see two ladies whom I recognised as members of the Dorian Trio exhibiting Llanarth Firefly, with whom they won a second prize!

The first breeding project at Blaenwern was when Firefly was mated to the Cardiganshire premium stallion Brenin Gwalia and Llanarth Vega was born in 1942. This mating was repeated and Llanarth Prince Roland was born in 1944; he was used in 1946 on Llanarth Fortress and Llanarth Rocket, dam of the great Llanarth Flying Saucer, was born in 1947. It was while driving along a lovely stretch of road by the River Wye near Builth Wells in 1945 that the Misses Taylor and Saunders Davies saw a roan two-year-old filly being ridden by small children, immediately fell for her and bought her. Although obviously of pure Welsh parentage, Fortress had no pedigree and was duly inspected and recorded as 'foundation stock', so Rocket became FS1 and Flying Saucer FS2. Rocket was the only filly which Fortress produced, and being only foundation stock, her colts could not be registered as entires, only as geldings, though some of the geldings became well-known performers such as Fortel, a favourite with disabled riders, and Beaufort a good winner in harness. Miss Taylor rode Fortress at the Display at the 1971 Royal Welsh Show during her year of Presidency and the loudest applause of the whole display came when I announced that the combined ages of horse and rider exceeded a century!

Rocket was sold as a riding pony to the Isle of Man after producing Flying Saucer, her one-and-only foal, in 1951. With Saucer having produced twenty foals including some of the 'greatest of all time', one wonders what would have happened had Rocket remained at Llanarth Stud.

Other additions to the Llanarth Stud in the forties were the colt, Llanarth Goldcrest, purchased from his breeder, Gwilym Morris of the Pistyll Stud (Pistyll Goldflake x Pistyll Sunset and foaled in 1945), and Llanarth Kilda (foaled in 1944), daughter of the noted Cardi Llwyd. The first of the famous animals to be bred at Llanarth was Llanarth Braint, foaled in 1948 as a result of the mating of Kilda to Goldcrest. Braint, progenitor of a dynasty at the Stud, almost was not born at Llanarth Stud at all since Kilda, in foal to Goldcrest in October 1947 was offered for sale at Llanybyther market but fortunately withdrawn when she failed to reach her modest reserve price of £30!

Llanarth Braint. Photo by Wynne Davies.

Llanarth Braint was not immediately accepted into the Cardiganshire Welsh Cob scene where the emphasis was on high-stepping harness trotting action, Cardiganshire bywords in the horse world being such names as 'Trotting Comet', 'High Stepping Gambler' and 'Trotting Jack'. Llanarth Braint was one of the first to enter the show ring fray with a long tail and compete under saddle at the canter and gallop. The Llanarth ladies sportingly travelled Braint outside the Principality to an audience who had never experienced such animals as Welsh Cobs. At the 1958 Ponies of Britain Show at Harrogate, Braint won the championship in hand, a first prize under saddle, another first in harness and the Supreme Championship of the whole show! This was not all – in the in-hand class the next five to him were all his progeny. He won the stallion class at the 1961 Royal Welsh Show and often stood second to his sons, such as Llanarth Brummel and Honyton Michael ap Braint. His greatest 'moment of glory' was probably at the 1969 Royal Agricultural Society of England Show where, at nineteen years of age, he put up the show of his life with Len Bigley (who had joined the stud in 1964 and was the same age as Braint) to stand champion Welsh Cob followed by various of his descendants of all ages and sexes.

Llanarth Braint's influence on the breed at Llanarth Stud was mainly through his daughter Llanarth Flying Saucer, whose own progeny included Llanarth Meteor (1959), winner of the harness championship at the 1972 Royal Welsh Show; Llanarth Flying Comet (1968), first prizewinner at the Royal Welsh Shows in 1969, 1970, 1971 and 1972 and champion in 1974, 1976, 1977 and 1978; Llanarth Flying Rocket (1969), a well-known producer; Llanarth Sian (1972), dam of the multi-champion Llanarth Sally; Llanarth Jack Flash (1976), champion in Australia, and many more.

Crossed with Rhosfarch Morwena, Llanarth Braint produced the 1970 Royal Welsh youngstock champion, Llanarth Meredith ap Braint, who also topped the 1979 WPCS sire ratings; Llanarth Marc ap Braint (1967), top sire in France; Llanarth Math ap Braint (1970), top sire in Canada; Llanarth Maldwyn ap Braint (1974), another top sire in Canada; Llanarth Mair (1975), top mare at Llanarth Stud and so on.

In 1961, Miss Saunders Davies left Blaenwern to go back to the Academy of Music and Miss Lewis bought the estate while continuing her career at the London Guildhall, requesting leave of absence annually to attend the Llanarth Sales, where she was a most gracious hostess. In

Llanarth Flying Comet held by Mr Len Bigley with the Royal Welsh Show George Prince of Wales Cup held by Miss Pauline Taylor (1974). Photo by Carole Knowles-Pfeiffer.

Llanarth Meredith ap Braint. Photo by Monty.

1976 Misses Taylor and Enid Lewis bequeathed Blaenwern Farm of 400 acres to the University College of Wales, Aberystwyth with the intention that a National Welsh Cob Stud for Wales would be maintained there for perpetuity. The University gained valuable publicity, since Llanarth Flying Comet had qualified for the Lloyds Bank Championship at the Horse of the Year Show six times, twice winning the championship (1979 and 1980) and appearing on national television. By 1980 Miss Taylor was worried that the stud was 'going the same way as the other College farms' and not as intended by the gift 'to foster the Welsh Cob for posterity', and a compromise University Stud Committee was set up, of which I was a member. The financial situation was eased in 1981 when the four-year-old stallion Llanarth Flyer was sold for a Welsh Cob record price and five foals were sold to the United States. Miss Enid Lewis died on 29 June 1980, followed by Miss Taylor on 17 June 1981; the agricultural side of Blaenwern had accumulated a big financial debt and the University decided to sell up. Various bodies objected to the sale, petitions were assembled all over the world, less drastic remedies were suggested; however the sale of the farm, most of the Cobs, cattle and sheep went ahead on 24 September 1983. One stallion, seven mares and two yearling fillies were retained on another farm for two years but subsequently they too were offered for sale by tender and fortunately rescued as one entity by Len and Anne Bigley, who by then were living at Michaelchurch Escley, Hereford.

The stallion was Llanarth Lord Nelson, foaled in 1979 and sired by Tyhen Comet out of Llanarth Lady Valiant and what a wonderful sire he has been at the Llanarth Stud of Mr Len Bigley (and Tregarth of Mrs Anne Bigley). When he was fourteen years old, he was taken away from his wives and broken to saddle, competing very successfully for two years, in fact qualifying for Olympia each year. Lord Nelson is well known for stamping his foals with his correct type, straight action and wonderful temperament.

The mares had good representation of the two most successful Llanarth matrons, Llanarth Flying Saucer and Rhosfarch Morwena. Flying Saucer's group were her daughter, Llanarth Sian (foaled in 1972) and Sian's daughter Llanarth Sally (foaled in 1976), who had won at the Royal Welsh Show as a yearling, two-year-old and three-year-old, as well as having won countless championships from the Royal Highland to Devon County, qualifying for Wembley four times. Sian went on to

Llanarth Lord Nelson, ridden by Catryn Bigley. Photo by Equestrian Services Thorney.

produce regularly (including Llanarth Trustful, a noted sire in the United States, foaled in 1985) until her death in 1993.

There were two daughters of Rhosfarch Morwena: Llanarth Morwena by Llanarth Braint, foaled in 1964 and Llanarth Marina by Llanarth Flying Comet, foaled in 1977, also Marina's daughter Llanarth Phoenix by Llanarth True Briton, foaled in 1983. Morwena also bred regularly until her death in 1988, her 1987 filly Llanarth Molly by Llanarth Lord Nelson being exported to Australia. Marina bred five foals between 1986 and 1990, her 1986 daughter Llanarth Nesta by Derwen Telynor proving to be a fantastic mare producing five fillies, all of whom have been retained as future brood mares. Phoenix has bred every year from 1987 to 1995, two of her foals being by the veteran Ceredigion Tywysog, which the Bigleys were so fortunate to lease from Fronarth Stud to keep this well-established bloodline going. Three of Phoenix's progeny have been exported, the 1987 filly Nansi to the United States, the 1992 filly, Empress, to Australia and the 1994 colt, Caredig, to Germany. Llanarth Meredid, bred by the University in 1982 and Rhosfarch Morwena's last foal (foaled when her dam was twenty-seven years old) had been sold to

Mrs Rothschild and was bought back by Len and Anne Bigley; she has produced a foal every year from 1989 to 1994, her 1994 colt Llanarth The Preacher by Ceredigion Tywysog is very highly thought of at Llanarth Stud, where it is intended for him to be the next main stud sire. Mererid was Overall Supreme Champion at the International Show, Compiegne, France in August 1996. Llanarth Stud in the ownership of Len and Anne Bigley is continuing along the lines set down by Miss Taylor, Miss Lewis and Miss Saunders Davies in 1943; they have won every major championship in the country and, although do not have such large numbers as at Blaenwern, are in great demand from all over the world, having exported ten animals since setting up at Michaelchurch Escley, three each to Australia and the United States, two to Germany and one each to Holland and Germany.

Nebo, Tyngwndwn

The start of the Nebo Stud could be regarded as being in 1961 when Geraint and Mary Jones were given by Geraint's father Idris Jones, of Tyngwndwn, Cross Inn, the three-year-old filly Tyngwndwn Mathrafal Lady with filly foal Nebo Fair Lady at foot, on the occasion of their marriage. But the foundations of the stud had been laid in 1918 when Geraint's grandfather Morgan Jones, Isfryn, Llanfarian bred Isfryn Bess by Creuddyn Welsh Flyer (g-g-son of Eiddwen Flyer – who was foaled in 1888) out of his 13-hand cream mare Gelmast Sally, daughter of Gelmast Peggy, who was sired by the noted Young King Jack. Tyngwndwn Beauty also was cream, sired by the North Cardiganshire premium stallion Cymro'r Wy and she had produced three fillies all sired by Brenin Gwalia: Tyngwndwn Bess (1943), Dolly (1944) and Malen (1946) dam of the influential Ceredigion Tywysog, then there was a gap of eleven years when she had another three foals, all sired by Mathrafal who was owned by Geraint's uncles, the Jones brothers of Fronarth Stud. The first of these, foaled in 1957 was the cream stallion Tyngwndwn Cream Boy, winner of the George Prince of Wales Cup in 1963; he was followed by Mathrafal Lady, then Tyngwndwn Prince in 1959 and her last foal (1960) was Tyngwndwn Llwyd o'r Glyn by Cahn Dafydd.

Nebo Fair Lady, the foal of the wedding present achieved fame by being the first Welsh Cob ever to fly across the Atlantic to the United States and I photographed her, looking less than half her age, at Mrs

Hope Garland Ingersoll's old-established Grazing Fields Stud in Massachusetts in 1980.

Mathrafal Lady's second foal (1962) was the noted Nebo Black Magic (Derwen Stud), George Prince of Wales Cup winner in 1973 and sire of the other champions Derwen Rosinda and Derwen Princess. Mathrafal Lady in 1963 produced Nebo Welsh Lady by Meiarth Royal Eiddwen and she went on to be an influential matron at the Nantcol and Trevallion Studs after producing Nebo Rosebud in 1968 by Rhystyd Prince. Rosebud (who died in 1994) had an enormous influence on the Nebo Stud and on the Welsh Cob breed in general. When Rosebud was two years old she was sent to Parc Welsh Flyer, duly producing Nebo Brenin. Brenin won his first WPCS premium at Lampeter as a four-year-old in 1975 and was proclaimed supreme champion of Lampeter Show in 1983, but his forté was in harness rather than in hand and he won amidst great applause in harness at the 1986 Royal Welsh Show. Nebo Brenin certainly made his mark as a sire; he was top of the WPCS sire-ratings in 1986, 1987, 1988, 1992 and 1993; his son Nebo Daniel took this premier place in 1989, 1990, 1994 and 1995, while Daniel's son, Nebo Prince (out of Daniel's g-dam Rosebud and therefore also maternal half-brother to Brenin), occupied this position in 1991 – so this trio have dominated the sire-ratings every year for a decade from 1986 to 1995. Daniel was retired at the 1990 Lampeter Show.

Nebo Princess Ann was Mathrafal Lady's 1973 foal (Hafrena Brenin) and she was greatly admired at twenty-two years old at the Nebo Stud's Open Day in June 1995, followed by her two great progeny the nineteen-year-old Nebo Daniel and the ten-year-old Nebo Princess Alice. Daniel was Royal Welsh Male champion in 1986, 1988 and 1989, winning the Prince of Wales Cup in 1988.

Princess Alice began her winning ways in youngstock classes, winning at the Royal Welsh and English Royal as a two-year-old and being champion at Ponies (UK) as a three-year-old. She won the Royal Welsh brood mare class in 1992 and, amidst nail-biting suspense within the top four places, ended up second in 1993 and 1995. Princess Alice's progeny are making their mark all over the world, her 1993 colt Nebo Dyfrig Express has taken Australia by storm for his owners John and Carole Riley of the Cwmkaren Stud in Queensland and the Belgian buyers of the 1995 filly Nebo Welsh Daffodil came over to admire her at the Open Day three months before she was weaned and exported. A turning point

Nebo Daniel, Overall Champion Royal Welsh Show 1988. Photo by Anthony Booth.

BELOW *Nebo Daniel on his retirement, Lampeter Show 1990. Photo by Carol Jones.*

in the development of Nebo Stud occurred in 1985 when Tewgoed Mari (foaled in 1981) was purchased from her breeder, the late Mr Hywel Williams at the Royal Welsh Sales. Mari was sired by Nebo Daniel out of Tewgoed Magic Lady who was by Nebo Black Magic out of the Tewgoed Stud's foundation mare Hewid Nesta. Tewgoed Mari's progeny at Nebo proved so outstanding that they immediately also secured her full sister (foaled in 1980) Tewgoed Janet and she is proving equally successful with such as Nebo Thomas (foaled in 1991) youngstock champion at the 1994 Royal Welsh Show.

Best known of Mari's progeny is Nebo Hywel by Nebo Brenin and foaled in 1987; he began his winning ways at the 1990 Lampeter Show where he won the Robleith Cup for the best three-year-old and later won three WPCS premiums there. Hywel's great moment of glory was at the 1994 Royal Welsh Show when he won the coveted Prince of Wales Cup and he was sold for a record figure in the spring of 1995 to Sam and Marie Sargant of Belvedere, Kent and immediately began winning championships for them in England.

Nebo Stud might not be the largest in recent years in terms of numbers kept but

Nebo Hywel at the Open Day, June 1995. Photo by Peter Hussey.

certainly it has had the greatest influence via usage of stallions; this fact was borne out at the 1995 Royal Welsh Sale when, of the 949 catalogued, no fewer than 126 claimed the 'Nebo' prefix for sire or dam's sire. There are not many Welsh Cob Studs which have not had an infusion of Nebo/Tyngwndwn blood somewhere along the way. Tyngwndwn Cream Boy spent most of his adult life with Eddie Price in Marlow and had a great influence on the breed in the South East of England, especially with harness Cobs. Nebo Black Magic sired the two invincible mares, Derwen Rosinda (foaled in 1970) and Derwen Princess (foaled in 1972), winners of the Prince of Wales Cup at the Royal Welsh Shows three times between them. Nebo Dafydd, foaled in 1970 (Brenin Dafydd x Tyngwndwn Mathrafal Lady), was senior sire at Cascob Stud for many years, producing such outstanding stock as Cascob Eluned (out of Nesscliffe Dallas by Tireinon Shooting Star) winner of a class of fifty-five yearling fillies at the 1989 Royal Welsh Show. Nebo Prince, foaled in 1980 (Nebo Daniel x Nebo Rosebud), has produced countless champions in hand, ridden and driven for the Navestock Stud in Brentwood, Essex. Tewgoed Magic Lady (daughter of Nebo Black Magic) topped the 1983 Derwen Sale and went to start Mr Strelin's Ruska Stud in Holland, her two daughters, Tewgoed Marind Tewgoed Janet, fortunately going back to Nebo to produce the 1994 Royal Welsh champion and youngstock champion Nebo Hywel and Nebo Thomas.

Ormond, Parc

There have been Welsh Cobs at Parc Stud since before Stud Book times. 535 Jolly II, foaled in 1894, a chestnut mare standing 15 hands was registered in volume I of the Welsh Stud Book, owned and bred by Samuel Davies of Coedparc, Derry Ormond, Lampeter. Jolly III was sired by Grand Express (a 15-hand chestnut) out of Jolly I by Wild Fire; g-dam Lettisha by Old Comet (foaled in 1840). Jolly II won first prizes at Lampeter Shows in 1895 and 1897 and a third in 1900. In 1917 Miss Rachel Davies, daughter of Samuel Davies was married to Mr D. O. Morgan, son of the Revd T. R. Morgan of Swyddffynnon and they took over the farming of Coedparc in 1919. The Welsh Cobs continued to be bred, first under the 'Ormond' prefix, which was later changed to 'Parc'. In 1927 D. O. Morgan bred Ormond Jolly (sired by Welsh Model out of Ormond Delight, daughter of the above Jolly II) and it was with her that he first competed in the show ring, winning at the Bath and West, Carmarthen and Gower and coming fourth at the Royal Welsh Show in 1931. Ormond Jolly's daughter by Cardigan Jack was foaled in 1936 and named Parc Delight. In the wartime years, Parc Delight produced Parc Welsh Maid, foaled in 1942 and sired by their own Parc Express (foaled in 1935 and a son of Ormond Jolly). Parc Welsh Maid deserves her place in any history of the Welsh Cob breed as dam of the legendary Parc Lady, foaled in 1948 and sired by Mathrafal. Parc Lady's Royal Welsh record of four times winning the George Prince of Wales Cup (1958, 59, 60 and 61) with an additional female championship (1956) will probably never be equalled.

D. O. Morgan judged the Welsh Cobs at the 1951 Royal Welsh Show. He was for many years a Council member of the WPCS, President during 1956/7 and later an Honorary Life Vice-President. Apart from his services to the WPCS, D. O. Morgan was a magistrate, a District Councillor, County Councillor and Alderman at the time of his death in 1965. D. O. Morgan was the first Chairman of the Lampeter Welsh Breeds Show, a position now held by his son, Sam Morgan, who joined the WPCS in 1948, has served on the Council since 1967 and was President in 1978/9.

Parc Welsh Maid had not been covered in 1947 and was exhibited at the first post-war Royal Welsh Show on 7 August, where she stood seventh in a class of ten mares all of which were well-known names in those days: Meiarth Welsh Maid, Dewi Rosina, Polly of Hercws, Oakford Charming Bess, Sheila, Daisy Gwenog, Parc Welsh Maid, Eiddwen's Pride, Phoebe of Trefecel and Princess Marina – in that order. Sam Morgan showing Parc Welsh Maid realised that she was in season at the show and there were the eight stallions present at the show, about the only eight stallions to survive the ravages of the war: Brenin Gwalia, Mathrafal, Meiarth Royal Eiddwen, Churchill, Brenin Cardi, Pistill Gold Flake, Cahn Dafydd and Tywysog Gwalia. Sam Morgan took a fancy to Mathrafal, a stallion which he had not seen since the 1938 Royal Agricultural Society of England Show at Cardiff, where he won the youngstock class and beat Sam's Parc Express for the male championship; arrangements were made to have Parc Welsh Maid covered at the Show by Mathrafal and the result in 1948 was the great Parc Lady.

Parc Lady with Mr Sam Morgan, Overall Champion Royal Welsh Show 1958. Photo by Wynne Davies.

The most successful crosses with Parc Lady were those using Pentre Eiddwen Comet (representing a total of eleven Royal Welsh championships between them, six male, five female and six supreme) and included Parc Comet (a good winner under saddle), Parc Prince (sold to the Argentine), Parc Pride, Parc Delight (one of the Cob foundation mares at Twyford Stud) and Parc Welsh Flyer. Parc Welsh Flyer was offered to Mr Cuneo of the United States for £250 in 1969 as part of a four-in-hand driving team, fortunately for the Welsh Cob breed there

*Parc Welsh Flyer. Photo by
Eberhard Holin.*

was a problem in matching up the fourth stallion and Parc Welsh Flyer,
one of the great sires from the seventies to the nineties remained in Wales
(he died in 1996), amongst his progeny being Nebo Brenin (five times
top of the WPCS section D sire ratings and nine times top of section C),
Craignant Flyer (sire of Mabnesscliffe Survivor, who sold for the highest
Welsh Cob price ever at the October sales, 10,400 guineas in 1988) and
fifteen sons and daughters including many champions out of Cathedine
Welsh Maid.

Parc Pride's most famous daughter was Parc Rachel, foaled in 1966,
sired by Cahn Dafydd and winner at the Royal Welsh as a foal, yearling,
two-year-old, three-year-old (Female Champion), winner of the George
Prince of Wales Cup three times in 1971, 1972 and 1975 and reserve for
overall championship in 1976 and 1978. In 1975 Parc Rachel qualified
for the Lloyd's In-Hand Championship at Wembley and appeared there
with another two Welsh Cob qualifiers, Llanarth Flying Comet and
Llanarth Meredith ap Braint. Parc Rachel died in 1989 but is represented

at Parc by two daughters, Parc Angharad (foaled in 1979 and sired by Parc Boneddwr) and Parc Roslin (foaled in 1987 and sired by Cippyn Red Flyer). Parc Reveller, son of Parc Angharad, foaled in 1986 and sired by Ebbw Victor was second to Pantanmlwg Red Fox out of sixty stallions at the 1991 Royal Welsh Show. He has been leased to Denmark. Parc Rachel's sons at Parc Stud are Parc Sir Ivor (foaled in 1977 and sired by Derwen Rosina's Last), sire of Ffoslas Lady Model the filly foal which sold for 4,200 guineas at the 1994 sale, Parc Cardi (foaled in 1984 and sired by Hewid Cardi) who was full-brother to Parc Brigadier whose record of 3,000 guineas at the 1980 Llanarth Sale held for eight years until Mabnesscliffe Survivor in 1988 and Parc Cardi was second and reserve male champion to Nebo Hywel at the 1994 Royal Welsh Show. Also standing at Parc Stud is Parc Rachel's last foal Parc Matador, foaled in 1988 and sired by Derwen Railway Express; his stock have already commanded high prices at sales.

Parc Rachel, Overall Champion Royal Welsh Show 1971

In addition to the noted Parc Rachel, Parc Pride also produced: (i) Parc Dafydd (foaled in 1964 and sired by Cahn Dafydd) who spent most of his life with Mrs Alison Mountain at the Twyford Stud in Sussex and who had a big influence on the Cobs of his native Cardiganshire through his big black son, Twyford Druid, stud stallion at Gwrthafarn Stud for many years; (ii) Parc Nest (foaled in 1969 and sired by Brenin Dafydd), sold to Mrs Deirdre Colville's Persie Stud from where her progeny went all over the world, for example, her son Persie Nimrod was a very successful sire at Mr Myburgh Streicher's Bukkenburg Stud in South Africa, where he is assisted in the stud duties by Parc Crusader (son of Rachel and Cyttir Telynor), exported to South Africa in 1986. When Mrs Colville dispersed her Persie Stud, Parc Nest was gladly welcomed back into her native county by Cerdin and Doreen Jones of the Synod Stud, her 1986 foal, Persie Nanette, coming here to Ceulan. Progeny (iii) was Parc Boneddwr (foaled in 1975, sired by Ceredigion Tywysog) who stood at stud at Parc until 1985 when he was exported to France and we have met some of his stock fetching top prices at sales, for example, Cathedine Pure Maid, who sold for 3,400 guineas in 1988. Undoubtedly the mare having the greatest influence on the present-day Parc Stud is Rachel's 1979 daughter Parc Angharad; two of her daughters sired by Parc Welsh Flyer were exported to the United States: Parc Ceridwen to Mrs Hope Ingersoll, Massachussetts in 1982 and Parc Maureen in 1986 to Gordon Heard, Virginia.

Two of Angharad's daughters retained at Parc are Parc Alice (foaled in 1987) by Nebo Daniel and Parc Gwenllian (1990) by Derwen Replica. Angharad's two-year-old daughter Parc Anest sired by Craignant Flyer was the eighth-highest female when sold for 2,600 guineas at the 1994 October sales. Daniel Morgan purchased Cathedine Margaret as a foal in 1985; she is one of the fifteen full-brothers and sisters of Parc Welsh Flyer x Cathedine Welsh Maid, and has produced six foals at Parc – three colts and three fillies. The Parc female line contains some of the most famous names in the breed back well into the last century and the family have chosen wisely by introducing some of the best outside sires e.g. Derwen Replica, Hewid Cardi, Ebbw Victor and Nebo Daniel. The aim is to retain the characteristics of the true Cardiganshire Welsh Cob and with this aim in mind, the Parc Stud has every chance of seeing their bloodlines progress into the next century. The future of the stud is secure with the next generation's three sons: Daniel, John and Richard.

Rhystyd, Pennal, Llwynhywel

The Rowlands Harris family of Mabwshen Farm, Llanrhystud near Aberystwyth in Dyfed have the unique distinction of breeding a continuous direct female line for well over a century. The members of the WPCS in volume 1 of the Welsh Stud Book in 1902 were the Rowlands Brothers, their kinsmen W. Rowlands of Brenan, New Cross, Aberystwyth being also members in volume 1 joined by R. Rowlands of Cwmhwylog, Nanteos, Aberystwyth in 1903. One of the animals bred by the Rowlands brothers in 1897 and registered in volume 1 of the Welsh Stud Book was Lady of Bute, sired by Alonzo II (son of Alonzo The Brave, chapter 1) out of Bess by Cardigan Flyer.

Lady of Bute was a prolific breeder but one daughter kept on at Rhystyd was Rhystyd Lady Horace, foaled in 1915 sired by Tregaron Horace and from her stems a continuous line down to Rhystyd Fashion (foaled in 1975), the foundation mare of the Pennal Stud.

Rhystyd Lady Horace was dam of Rhystyd Flashlight (foaled in 1922) sired by Rhystyd Comet

she was dam of Rhystyd Rosina			foaled in 1928	sired by	Trotting Jack
who was	..	Tit Bit	 1938	..	.. Rhystyd Trustee
.. ..	..	Queen	 1946	..	.. Brenin Gwalia
.. ..	..	Lady Model	 1951	..	.. Pentre Eiddwen Comet
.. ..	..	Lively Maid	 1964	..	.. Brenin Gwalia
.. ..	..	Fashion	 1975	..	.. Llanarth Meredith ap Braint

---

The three Rowlands brothers living at Mabwshen in 1902 were David, Lewis and William, three bachelors – but they had a sister, Annie, who married Thomas Harris of Llechryd in South Cardiganshire and it was their son Daniel Rowlands Harris who inherited Mabwshen and continued the Rhystyd Stud.

Daniel Rowlands Harris in 1922 married Jane Emily James of Perthygwenyn, Llanrhystud and they had five children between 1923 and 1935, the three bachelor sons David, James and Gwynne staying on at Mabwshen. Margaret (Mrs Williams) lived nearby and William married Mary Ann James of Llanerchpentir, Crosswood, in 1957 then moving to farm at Esgairsaeson, Blaenpennal, Aberystwyth where he was to carry on the Rhystyd bloodlines under the 'Pennal' prefix, assisted by their son

Dafydd, who is farming Esgairsaeson, and daughter Jane (Mrs Evans) who, with her husband David, has adopted the 'Llwynhywel' prefix.

Another family of Cobs bred at Mabwshen in those early days was Trustful Princess, a 15-hand brown daughter of Trustful out of Darby by Welsh Flyer, and she was foaled in 1903. But it is the Lady of Bute foundation which has survived at Rhystyd Stud to win Royal Welsh Show championships, fetch top prices at sales and provide the foundation for many of the leading present-day studs. Eight silver WPCS medals were won in the period up to 1930 at such Shows as Llanilar, Llangeitho, Tregaron, Aberystwyth and Lampeter with the Cobs shown in hand, under saddle and in harness after having been ridden or driven to the showground.

It was at the 1968 Royal Welsh Show that the Rhystyd prefix really hit the big time. Although there were only seventy-one entries in the whole Welsh Cob section of seven classes, great names were present in abundance; Parc Rachel, who was later to win five Royal Welsh championships, won the filly class, while the 1969 champion, Tyhen Comet, won the colt class. The overall champion was the mare class winner, Derwen Rosina, winning for the third time in her short life and the 'Rhystyd' victor was the stallion winner and male champion, Rhystyd Prince, owned by Kenneth Price and he had beaten Brenin-y-Bryniau, the 1970 champion Brenin Dafydd, the 1967 champion Honyton Michael ap Braint, Golden Sunshine, son of the 1962 champion Pentre Rainbow and the old warrior, the six-times winner but now twenty-two years old, Pentre Eiddwen Comet, in that order.

Rhystyd Prince was foaled in 1960, sired by Brenin Gwalia out of Rhystyd Lady Model, who was foaled in 1951 and sired by Pentre Eiddwen Comet out of Rhystyd Queen by Brenin Gwalia. It was Rhystyd Lady Model who had the greatest influence on current bloodlines at the Rhystyd Stud; apart from Rhystyd Prince, amongst her fifteen Rhystyd progeny are Rhystyd Welsh Maid (f. 1959) dam of the great Brenin Brynawelon, Rhystyd Actress (foaled in 1962), producer of exceptional stock at the Gerrig Stud, Rhystyd Lively Maid (foaled in 1964), dam of Rhystyd Frenin, the big winner at the Pipers Green Stud – before being exported to Germany – and the great Rhystyd Fashion, who we shall meet later, Rhystyd Bouncing Lady (foaled in 1968) dam of the 1979 Royal Welsh male champion Rhystyd Meredith and Rhystyd Mattie (foaled in 1973), the first Welsh Cob to sell for 2,000

ABOVE *Brenin Brynawelon, son of Rhystyd Welsh Maid, driven by Mr Peter Gray.*

Rhystyd Fashion. Photo by Ceri Davies.

Rhystyd Meredith, Male Champion Royal Welsh Show 1979. Photo by Ceri Davies.

guineas at auction (2,300 guineas on the 1978 Llanarth Sale) – a female record which was to hold for another nine years.

Rhystyd bloodlines therefore were a mainstay in the formation of many of the leading studs of the day such as Gerrig, Brynawelon Thorneyside, Okeden and many others. When the Mabwshen brothers offered the yearling filly Rhystyd Fashion for sale (lot 164) at the 1976 Llanarth Sale, she created a great deal of interest; not only was she a very elegant filly but she was sired by the successful Llanarth Meredith ap Braint and her dam, Rhystyd Lively Maid, was full-sister to the Royal Welsh champion, Rhystyd Prince. Other brother William Harris of Esgaersaeson was very wise to buy her at 600 guineas, which was the top yearling price of the sale. Rhystyd Fashion was soon to make her mark in the show ring; as a two-year-old she was the champion filly at Lampeter and at three won her class at the Royal Welsh and stood reserve female champion – a rare feat for a youngster. As a brood mare, Fashion came so close to winning the Royal Welsh many times (second in 1979, 1982, 1983 and third in 1984), however she deserves her name in history for what she produced and she is the only mare to have produced four winners of the foal class at the Royal Welsh. One of her Royal Welsh winning daughters, who also won as a yearling, was Pennal Lady May by

Parc Welsh Flyer, who proved a great advertisement for the Welsh Cob breed in South Africa.

Her 1982 foal Pennal Lady Model by Parc Dafydd has produced two October sale toppers, Pennal Calon Lan by Tynged Calon Lan top-priced colt foal (1,000 guineas) at the 1988 sale and Pennal Confidence, colt foal by Tireinon Confidence who fetched the highest male price of any age (2,600 guineas) at the 1995 sale. Pennal Calon Lan himself is making his mark at the Abergavenny Stud. Despite being only seven years old in 1995 his three-year-old daughter Abergavenny Welsh Model was the highest-priced section D (4,000 guineas) at the Royal Welsh Sale.

Pennal Calon Lan. Photo by Wynne Davies

Rhystyd Fashion's death in 1995 was a great loss to the breed but her daughters are carrying on the strain, which has been in the family for over a century. After she died in the summer, her foal at foot Pennal Fashion's Delight by Parc Reveller was introduced to the show ring and won the reserve championship to the stallion Parc Cardi at Llanddewi Brefi Show. There are four breeding mares of the same strain still at Mabwshen and at Llwynhywel Stud, so the foundations laid by the

Rowlands Brothers at the beginning of the Welsh Pony and Cob Society are continuing in safe hands.

Thorneyside

It was in 1973 that Mr Peter Gray joined the WPCS and established the Thorneyside Stud at Moorwards Farm, Iver Heath, Buckinghamshire. Several generations of his ancestors had been heavily involved with harness horses and Peter Gray to this day owns some of the best trotters and Hackneys in Britain, such as Holmfield Narrator, the 1990 Royal Welsh champion and 1994 reserve champion. It is not surprising, therefore, that when he came to select some Welsh Cobs for his stud that it was those with plenty of fire and dash which found favour, a characteristic for which the Thorneyside Cobs have become famous and which won for them major championship awards, top prices at sales and an enviable export trade.

In the 1960s Peter Gray's father bought the Cob stallion Llwnog-y-Gwendraeth from Mr John Thomas of the Gwendraeth Stud, Kidwelly, Dyfed; he was a son of the great 'goer' Llwynog-y-Garth and had plenty of bone and substance, using his joints to great effect. This was the stamp of Welsh Cob which Peter Gray had at the back of his mind when he set up his own stud in the early seventies, his first purchase being the black stallion Ross Black Prince, foaled in 1968. Black Prince was in fact registered in section C but examination of his extended pedigree reveals a preponderance of section D blood, and real 'blue' blood at that; no wonder that two Royal Welsh champions were bred at Thorneyside only two generations from Black Prince himself. Black Prince was sired by Tyssul Valiant (foaled in 1962) by Prince Valiant, a son of Queenie, seven times section C Royal Welsh champion between 1947 and 1961. Tyssul Valiant's dam was a top-class Cob mare, Goyan Black Bess (foaled in 1941), daughter of Oakford Black Bess by the immortal Ceitho Welsh Comet. Black Prince's dam was Faelog Frolic, Royal Welsh section C female champion in 1979, who hailed from many generations of breeding at Llanfaelog, Penuwch, the village which has had more influence on Welsh Cob history than any other in the Principality.

The first mare at Thorneyside was Regency Raindrop, bred by the pioneer England Welsh Cob stalwart, Eddie Price of Marlow. Raindrop was foaled in 1971, sired by the 1963 Royal Welsh Cup winner,

Tyngwndwn Cream Boy. The first Cob mare bred at Thorneyside was Thorneyside Flying Lady (foaled in 1975) by Ross Black Prince out of Regency Raindrop; she has the unique distinction of having bred two Royal Welsh male champions, full brothers Thorneyside The Boss (champion in 1990) and Thorneyside Flyer (1992).

The Boss and Flyer are sired by Brynymor Welsh Magic, sired by Nebo Black Magic out of Hwylog Briallen. Welsh Magic had won his class at the Royal Welsh Show in 1974, again repeating this success in 1976 and going on to be reserve male champion to Llanarth Flying Comet – and so it was quite a coup for Thorneyside to buy him from Derwen Stud in 1979.

Prior to the purchase of Brynymor Welsh Magic, the senior stallion at Thorneyside had been Brenin Bynawelon, purchased privately from Mr and Mrs Dennis Bushby of the Buckswood Stud at the 1975 Llanarth Sale. Brenin Brynawelon was foaled in 1968, sired by Hendy Brenin out of Rhystyd Welsh Maid, she being full-sister to the 1968 Royal Welsh champion Rhystyd Prince. He had been bought by Buckswood Stud as a foal and had sired many good mares there, probably the best known of which is Buckswood Elegant Lady. Brenin Brynawelon was a noted

Thorneyside The Boss, Male Champion Royal Welsh Show 1990 at home with Mr Peter Gray. Photo by Trevor Newbrook.

winner in hand and harness for Thorneyside, winning in harness at the Royal Welsh Show for the last time in 1987 (at nineteen years old) but also proving to be a wonderful sire. Thorneyside Fashion was a daughter, foaled in 1980 out of Thorneyside Flying Lady, the dam of The Boss and Flyer. Fashion herself became the dam of Thorneyside The Wizard, a multiple winner in hand, Lampeter winner, Thorneyside The Gaffer, the most consistent winner in South Wales during 1995, Thorneyside The Guvnor and the 1995 Royal Welsh and Lampeter winner, Thorneyside The Gladiator.

The progeny of Thorneyside stallions are in great demand at the society sales. Brynymor Welsh Magic had been leased to Synod Stud in 1986 and his daughter Synod Rosary was sold to Fronarth as a foal for 1,450 guineas, twice as much as any other filly foal sold. The yearling colt Thorneyside Echo (Thorneyside The Boss x Dolygarn Cariad) was the highest-priced yearling (1,500 guineas) at the 1988 sales and Thorneyside More Magic (at four years, Brynymor Welsh Magic x Thorneyside Welsh Maid) topped the 1989 sale at 6,000 guineas to Paul Davies of Llanelli. Thorneyside Spring Magic (Brynymor Welsh Magic x Thorneyside Melody by Brenin Brynawelon) set a new record in 1990 of 3,500 guineas for a yearling colt selling to octogenarian Hans Strelin of Holland where he died in 1995. This record was broken in 1992 when 5,000 guineas was paid for the yearling colt Thorneyside The Gaffer (Derwen Telynor x Thorneyside Fashion by Brenin Brynawelon). Thorneyside Norma Jean (Thorneyside Flyer x Thorneyside Magic Maid) has made the long trip to Australia where she will be an excellent ambassador for the breed.

Thorneyside Welsh Cobs have had enormous successes in the show ring, The Boss winning a class of 73 stallions at the 1990 Royal Welsh Show and male championship from the Three Counties and Lampeter champion Cathedine Express, the 1991 Royal Welsh champion Pantanamlwg Red Fox and Sydenham Stud's Llanarth Lloyd George. Flyer repeated this achievement from a class of fifty-eight in 1992 from the sales record-holder Mabnesscliffe Survivor, the 1983 and 1984 Royal Welsh male champion Ebbw Victor and the 1993 champion Horeb Euros. The only Welsh Cob to qualify in ten years for the Lloyds Bank/Creber/Templeton competition at Wembley was Nebo Daniel (Three Counties Show, 1987) but The Boss came reserve twice in 1990 and Flyer twice in 1995 (Royal Cornwall and Royal Norfolk); then The

Thorneyside Flyer, Male Champion Royal Welsh Show 1992 with Mr Len Bigley.

Boss's son, the six-year-old Synod Rambo qualified at Cheshire County in 1996, the following year selling for 10,000 guineas at the Royal Welsh Sales.

Mr Peter Gray has generously allowed his champion stallions to spend some years in Wales; already mentioned was Brynymor Welsh Magic who was at Synod Stud in 1986. The two Royal Welsh champion sons then spent two years each at Synod Stud, Thorneyside The Boss in 1988 and 1989 and Thorneyside Flyer in 1990 and 1991. Many of the top Welsh studs took advantage of being able to use the Thorneyside stallions while they were in Wales; there are three exceptional daughters of Flyer at the Gwynfaes/Penllwynuchel Stud and two Flyer daughters were greatly admired at the Fronarth Stud Open Day in June 1995. These were Fronarth Miss Magic (foaled in 1991), the youngest of the brood mares on view that day and her full-sister (foaled in 1992), both out of Fronarth Brenhines; she was Fronarth Cymraes who had won at Lampeter as a yearling. Son John, a former champion Young Handler at Northleach and the Royal Welsh, is just as interested in the Cobs as his father – so the future of the Thorneyside Stud is in safe hands.

CHAPTER EIGHT

The Welsh Cob part bred

SOME FAMOUS horses of the past, including Grand National and Badminton winners, had Welsh Cob blood in their veins but were usually not credited as such, so in 1960 a 'Welsh Part-bred Register' was included at the back of Volume 43 of the Welsh Stud Book to record ponies with 25 per cent of Welsh pony blood and horses with 25 per cent of Welsh Cob blood. The 25 per cent need not come from one source (that is, one grandfather or grandmother); it can be cumulative – for instance, one great-grandfather plus one great-grandmother, not necessarily on the same side, or any other combinations from ancestors further back which, when added together, result in a total of 25 per cent which sometimes is a combination of pony and Cob blood. Part-bred horses and ponies will increase their percentage of Welsh blood when crossed with pure Welsh sires or used on pure Welsh dams, however, even if a percentage approaches one hundred per cent, the progeny will always remain in the Part-Bred Register and never be allowed back into the Stud Book proper.

The first attempt at establishing the Welsh Part-Bred Register in 1960 attracted only one stallion, eight mares and twelve geldings; however, in the intervening years, Welsh part-bred ponies and Cobs have become very popular and successful. Of the total of 8,580 registrations processed for sections A, B, C, D and part-breds during 1995, 1,506 (17 per cent) were for the part-bred register.

The reason why experimenting with outside crosses on Welsh Cob mares got off to a slow start was the dearth of pure-bred females available, their numbers having been depleted to dangerously low numbers during the second World War. The eight stallions, ten mares and seven young-stock competing at the 1947 Royal Welsh Show (compared with 542 in

1995) represented most of the available animals in Britain at that time. Ten years later the situation had improved somewhat – though not dramatically – and the pioneers in the breeding of Welsh Cob part-breds were Lt Colonel and Mrs Ivor Reeves of Moreton-in-the-Marsh, Gloucestershire who, in 1958, purchased the sixteen-year-old Welsh Cob mare Camp Polly, whose pedigree contained some of the most famous names within the breed. In 1959 Camp Polly was served by the HIS stallion Question producing M'Dear (50 per cent) in 1960. M'Dear went on to produce a whole host of noted Welsh part-bred hunters (25 per cent) such as Bee's Wax, sired by the HIS stallion, Flying Bee. To speed up their Welsh part-bred breeding programme, Colonel and Mrs Reeves then purchased the Welsh part-bred mare Heather, sired by Avaunt GSB out of the Welsh Cob mare Hafrena Queen by Llanarth Braint. The same year that M'Dear produced Bee's Wax by Flying Bee, Heather produced Bee's Wing by the same sire. Bee's Wing was sold to Ted Edgar who re-named him Everest Jet Lag and he won the Schroder Life Jumping Competition at the 1978 Horse of the Year Show. In 1979 Everest Jet Lag was ridden by HRH The Prince of Wales to win a major competition at Olympia.

Colonel and Mrs Reeves then experimented with producing part-breds the 'other way round' and achieved equal, possibly even great success. The Welsh Cob stallion Llanarth Brummel (1964 and 1965 Royal Welsh champion) lived nearby at the Sydenham Stud and he was sired by Llanarth Braint, who had already proved successful as a producer of good performers for Colonel and Mrs Reeves. Llanarth Brummel crossed onto the Reeves's Thoroughbred mare, Pleasant Fancy, produced Palm Fancy, whose progeny by other Thoroughbreds include The Prince (who measured over 17 hands), Game Fair, who was successful in Britain and later in Switzerland and Palm Fair, who was overall champion hunter at the North Buckinghamshire Show. A more recent product of this family was Lord Lawrence the 1986 in-hand champion at the Royal Welsh Show. Welsh Cob part-breds from the Llanarth Braint families were also bred at the Llanarth Stud in Cardiganshire; the Llanarth Braint daughter Llanarth Ebony was sent several times to Mr and Mrs Gilbert's Thoroughbred stallion Nerium at Newcastle Emlyn. The progeny of this mating included Llanarth Nerissa (foaled in 1971), Llanarth Natasha who went to Holland (Mr and Mrs Poldervaart), Llanarth Natalie (sold to Mr and Mrs Derek Gethin as a brood mare for their HIS stallions) and Llanarth Neruda who is a dressage horse at Grand Prix level.

Llanarth Nerissa was given to Mrs Anne Bigley on the occasion of her marriage to the Llanarth Stud partner Len Bigley and her progeny are phenomenal:

1977 Daisy Hill by Hill Farmer, owned by Mr and Mrs Derek Gethin, in 1987 she was champion hunter brood mare at both the Royal Agricultural Society of England and Royal Welsh Shows.

1978 Maritime by Marine Corps, she was top-priced yearling when bought by Geoffrey Buckingham-Bawden at the Hunter Sales and won championships in hand, under saddle and later as a brood mare.

1980 Magical Air by Current Magic, another winner in youngstock classes but tragically had to be put down when young during a foaling accident.

1981 Magical Touch again by Current Magic, now known as Schubert, he is a successful Advanced dressage horse.

1982 Hill Street Blues by Hill Farmer, a successful showjumper.

1983 Better by Design by Better by Far, a good producer including the top lot at the 1992 Festival of the Horse.

1985 Portobello by Mart Lane, a good hunter, grew to 18 hands.

1986 Petticoat Lane by Mart Lane, very successful in hand and under saddle.

1987 April Folly by Big Ivor, dam of the top-priced foal at the 1992 Festival of the Horse for the Langarth Stud.

1988 Smithfield again by Mart Lane, sold for eventing.

1991 Swansong by Hubble Bubble, retained at Llanarth Stud since her dam had to be put down suffering from cancer when Swansong was six weeks old.

The achievements of this family illustrate the versatility of Welsh Cob part-breds and some of the following are animals which have become household names in the horse world:

Showjumpers

Brooke Street April Sun   16 hands 2 in grey gelding, foaled in 1978, bred by Mr W. D. Green, Haverfordwest, Dyfed. His sire was the HIS stallion Harvest Sun and his dam, April Dawn, was sired by another HIS stallion, Rice Pudding out of the Welsh Cob mare, Bess. Ridden by Robert Smith in 1987, he won £16,000 in six weeks. Total winnings (BSJA): £89,755.

Mushki Brummel   16-hand roan gelding, sired by Llanarth Brummel. An international Grade A showjumper, previously ridden by Robert Smith and later by Tracey Priest.

Harden Dilwyn   15 hands 2 in, chestnut gelding, foaled in 1975, sired by the Welsh Cob stallion, Dilys Golden Harp (Parc Dafydd x Golden Gem) out of the GSB mare Copse. He was fourth in the 1991 Hickstead Derby and, ridden by Tracey Priest, has gained a place in the Great Britain Nations Cup team every year from 1989 to 1992, for which he was awarded the Brodrick Memorial trophy at the 1992 WPCS Annual General Meeting.

Mister Woppit   16 hands 2 in, bay gelding, foaled in 1990, his WPCS name is Penlanganol Jasper and he was bred by Mr and Mrs Terry Jones of Penlanganol, Cribyn, sired by the 15 hands 3 in liver chestnut stallion Maesmynach Viking Warrior, his dam is the Thoroughbred mare KC, whose sire is Hustler. He was sold at the 1993 Festival of the Horse and, ridden by Ian Wynne, has won £537 in two years showjumping, which won for him the title Welsh Part-Bred Premiere Champion of 1995. By the end of 1997 Mister Woppit, who is now BSJA Grade 'A', has won £3,867, gaining for his sire Maesmynach Viking Warrior the British Horse Foundation award for the show-jumping sire gaining most progeny points. This is the first time that a 'Native' stallion has won a British Horse Foundation award.

Event horses

Garmon Cerise   15 hands 2 in chestnut mare, sired by the Welsh Cob stallion Llanarth Brenin Siarl out of the Thoroughbred mare La Corrida. In 1988 she was selected for the British Junior Championships Windsor Three Day Event and won the Range Rover Young Rider Bursary at

ABOVE *Mushki Brummel at the Horse of the Year Show. Photo by MVR Photographic.*

Harden Dilwyn ridden by Tracey Priest. Photo by Elizabeth Furth.

Mister Woppit (Penlanganol Jasper) ridden by Ian Wynn. Photo by Fotograffs.

BELOW *Shilling of Knoxfauld, ridden by David Herron. Photo by Neil B Jones.*

Garmon Cerise ridden by Shell Attfield. Photo by Equestrian Services Thorney.

Gatcombe in 1992. Now retired to stud. Garmon Cerise was bred by Mrs M McIlveen, Nant Ganol, Capel Garmon, Llanrwst, Gwynedd.

Shilling of Knoxfauld   16 hands chestnut gelding, foaled in 1987, sired by the Welsh Cob stallion, Scole Herbert (by Llanarth Welsh Warrior) out of Penny Arden by Ardencaple (GSB). Shilling was bred by Mrs Macgregor of Dunblane, Perthshire, Scotland and owned and ridden by David Herron of Northumberland. Shilling has won over £400 in BSJA Showjumping and also been very successful in horse trials, collecting 123 BHS Horse Trial points. In 1994 he won the senior individual award in the Pony Club Horse Trials championships and the Weston Park Advanced Horse Trials in 1995.

Another Late Nite   Bay gelding, foaled in 1979, sired by the Welsh Cob stallion Garmon Pelydryn Aur (Golden Sunshine x Fronarth Gwenllian) out of Sidan (PBAR) by Akbar Krakus. His registered Welsh part-bred name is Montego's Frère D'Aimée. He was bred by Mr Strongetharm, Amlwch, Gwynedd and now owned by Harriet Saunders, Faringdon, Oxford, who purchased him on Bonfire Night and the transport broke down on his way home, hence his change of name. They have competed successfully at Windsor, Bramham, and Blenheim International Three-

Bushbaby, Advanced Dressage Horse. Photo by Pleasure Prints.

Comedy ridden by Mrs Jo Fletcher. Photo by Equestrian Services Thorney.

197

Day Events, also won the Heythrop Pony Club Two-Day Event in 1995 and various other One-Day Events.

Dressage horses

Bushbaby   15 hands 2 in grey gelding by Sage Baby, who has a Welsh Cob grand-dam (daughter of Llanarth Braint). He was bred by Mr D. Thomas at Llanybyther. In 1989 he was second at the National Dressage Championships and has 261 dressage points.

Comedy   15-hand bay gelding, foaled in 1976 and sired by the 1966 and 1969 Royal Welsh champion Welsh Cob stallion Tyhen Comet out of the HIS mare, Honesty by Sable Skinflint. Comedy was bred by K. and L. Newey at Balsall Common, near Coventry but has been owned since

Westwell Prim and Proper ridden by Charlotte Down. Photo by Pleasure Prints.

1981 by Mrs Jo Fletcher of Mitchell's End, Solihull who rides him. Horse and rider learnt everything about dressage together, culminating with 375 dressage points, and hence qualifying for the National Championships at Goodwood House in 1991.

Westwell Prim and Proper a 15-hand bay mare, foaled in 1980 and sired by Ben Faerie (TB) out of the Welsh Cob mare, Pipers Green Celebration by Dilys Golden Rain (Pentre Rainbow x Golden Gem by Llanarth Braint). Prim and Proper was bred by Mrs P. M. Williams of Westwell Farm, Shepton Mallet and broken in by her daughter, well-known event rider Caroline Keevil, and then sold to her present owner Mrs Julia Down of Frome in 1985. Prim and Proper has had many successes in dressage competitions, ridden by Mrs Down, as well as eventing, ridden by daughters Charlotte Down and Lis Trott, winning the Pony Club Horse Trials Championships in 1989.

Welsh Cob part-breds have also been exceptionally successful as harness animals. George Bowman originally won the world gold medal, driving four pure-bred Welsh Cobs (three of them bred at Scole Stud) but more recently has been driving part-bred 'Cumberland' Cobs. Ewald Welde from Austria has also been competing in International Driving competitions, driving a pair of Welsh Cob x Kladruber geldings. Mrs Gidley-Wright's chestnut driving horse Naf Naf's Major Joseph, winner of ten championships in 1991–4 is a Welsh Cob x Arab gelding.

Index of horse names

MORE BOOKS ON HORSES FROM J. A. ALLEN

The Horse Breakers
Clive Richardson

This fascinating book details the work of horse whisperers, gentlers, rough-riders, charlatans and showmen over many centuries, together with the methods of present-day masters, like Monty Roberts. The book traces man's involvement with the domestication of the horse from its origins in Persia 8,000 years ago to the present day. It covers the evolution of horse-breaking methods across a diversity of cultures and looks at the folklore, mythology and mysticism that built up around these men.

9 x 6 in: 200 pages approx: black and white photographs and line illustrations:
ISBN 0.85131.722.7: **£19.95 June**

The Veterinary Care of the Horse
Sue Devereux, MRCVS and Liz Morrison, LLB, BHSII

A complete veterinary handbook for the horse owner written in simple language in an inviting and concise format designed for easy reference. Illustrated with profuse line illustrations and photographs collected from a busy equine practice, this book is an invaluable aid for anyone needing to know exactly how to care for a sick or injured horse and wishing to gain a better understanding of modern veterinary practice.

9½ x 7½ in: 245 pages: photographs and line illustrations: ISBN 0.85131.543.7: **£19.95**

First Foal
Jane van Lennep

Experienced stud owner Jane van Lennep describes the pleasures and perils of breeding a foal and takes the reader step-by-step through the whole process from an evaluation of the mare and choice of stallion to the care of the foal in the first few vital hours. Illustrated with superb colour photographs. Jane van Lennep's reassuring and easy-to-read text will help assuage the fears of the most apprehensive first-time breeder.

9¼ x 8½ in: 112 pages: profuse colour photographs: ISBN 0.85131.532.1: **£15.95**

First Steps
Jane van Lennep

A complete guide to the care, handling and management of foals, yearlings and youngstock including advice on ailments and showing written by a successful stud owner and show ring exhibitor. Full of lovely colour photographs and a companion to *First Foal*.

9¼ x 8½ in: 178 pages: profuse colour photograph: ISBN 0.85131.619.0: **£18.95**

Equine Welfare
Marthe Kiley-Worthington

This book outlines the history of equine welfare and investigates the conventional practices of horse management and training. It examines the degree to which equines may suffer in the competitive disciplines and looks at their role in hunting, riding schools, rodeo and circuses. Many of the points the book raises are controversial but it is hoped that it will bring about a change for the improvement of life for all equines.

9¼ x 6¼ in: photographs and line illustrations: cloth: ISBN 0.85131.704.9: **£19.95**

The Holistic Management of Horses
Keith Allison with Christopher Day, MRCVS

A practical guide to the everyday management of the horse prepared for the increasing number of owners who wish to apply the philosophy of holism to the care of horses, working in harmony with natural principles rather than against them. The benefits, the theory and the practice of this natural and humane approach to horse care are fully explained and illustrated.
Published in association with the British Association of Holistic Nutrition and Medicine.

9½ x 6¼ in: 200 pages: line and photographic illustrations: ISBN 0.85131.623.9: **£17.95**